Fixing Russia's Banks

T0164095

Fixing Russia's Banks
A Proposal for Growth

Michael S. Bernstam
and
Alvin Rabushka

HOOVER INSTITUTION PRESS

Stanford University   Stanford, California

URL: http://www-hoover.stanford.edu

Hoover Institution Press Publication No. 449
Copyright © 1998 by the Board of Trustees of the
Leland Stanford Junior University

First printing, 1998
04   03   02   01   00   99   98   9   8   7   6   5   4   3   2   1

Manufactured in the United States of America

The paper used in this publication meets the minimum requirements
of American National Standard for Information Sciences—Permanence
of Paper for Printed Library Materials, ANSI Z39.48–1984. ⊗

Library of Congress Cataloging-in-Publication Data
Bernstam, Mikhail S.
  Fixing Russia's banks : a proposal for growth /
Michael S. Bernstam and Alvin Rabushka.
      p.   cm.
  Includes bibliographical references and index.
  ISBN 0-8179-9572-2 (alk. paper)
  1. Banks and banking—Russia (Federation)   2. Monetary policy—
Russia (Federation)   3. Russia (Federation)—Economic
conditions—1991–   I. Rabushka, Alvin.   II. Title.
HG3130.2.A6B476   1998
332.1'0947—dc21   98-22972
                                                            CIP

CONTENTS

INTRODUCTION

Since the breakup of the Soviet empire in 1991, Russia has attempted but failed to develop a real market economy. The Russian economy has experienced a massive (40 percent) contraction in national income and consumption. Opportunities for sustained growth have been derailed by repeated failures of economic policy. The ostensible major economic reforms that were carried out—privatization, removal of price controls, foreign trade liberalization, reducing inflation—did not generate the widely expected prosperity.[1]

The Coming Russian Boom,[2] the title of a book written in 1996, reflects a widely held view that economic growth in Russia

1. The authors would like to thank Thomas E. MaCurdy of the Hoover Institution and Department of Economics, Stanford University, for his valuable insights that we incorporated throughout this volume. Yakir Plessner, professor of economics at Hebrew University (Rehovot), and Andrew I. Sitnikov, of the Institute of Systems Analysis of the Russian Academy of Sciences, provided seminal ideas, institutional knowledge, and useful comments on various segments of this book. Those scholars do not necessarily agree with all of our analyses and conclusions. We alone are responsible for the content of the volume.

2. Richard Layard and John Parker, *The Coming Russian Boom* (New York: Free Press, 1996).

is inevitable. That inevitability is found in the country's highly educated population, the high savings rate of its people, and, most important, its vast natural resources, especially oil, gas, and strategic metals. In addition, Russia appears to have made perceptible progress in attaining macroeconomic stability by bringing inflation under control.

So why has the *boom* not yet come? The explanation lies, in large measure, in Russia's failure to develop a financial system independent of the government, specifically, a real commercial banking system, which is an essential component of a market economy. To redress that problem, we set forth a proposal for reforming Russia's financial markets that strives to establish a real banking system.

The central theme of this book is simply put. Compared with Western market economies, banks in the Russian Federation (hereafter Russia) do not engage in normal banking practices of accepting deposits and making loans, do not facilitate normal investment, and therefore do not contribute to growth. *Russian banks are not really banks at all.* They have the look and feel of banks but are better described as nonbank banks or pseudobanks—we prefer the term *ersatz,* or *inferior imitation, banks.* Their owners and managers may use the name *banks,* but these institutions are not banks. Rather, they have served since 1991 as financial arms of the government and the Central Bank of Russia, distributing and reallocating resources to favored individuals, companies, groups, and industries. They play a role in economic development but one unique to Russia and similar countries, in that the banks themselves are the principal instruments of ownership, management, and subsidies and are the chief beneficiaries of the transition. This strategy has not yet brought visible economic improvement to the rank and file of the Russian people.

Why do we attach such importance to banks? Apart from their

normal role of allocating resources by accepting deposits from the public and making loans to enterprises, banks also establish clear boundaries between the "public" and the "private." A defining characteristic of socialism is the unity, commonality, or indivisibility of the public and private. Under socialism, all resources were owned or controlled by the state and all production was financed by the state. A starting point of transition economies is to create private ownership and separate the financing of production from the government. The establishment of real commercial banks, independent of the government, becomes the vehicle to break up the financial chain of socialism. Banks create the sovereignty of private individuals in the economy by lifting households to the role of reigning lenders, thereby replacing the government, which is relegated to a more limited role of issuing money and performing other legitimate public endeavors.

The book has four chapters. Chapter 1 provides some background material on Russian economic conditions. Chapter 2 covers 1991–1995, what we term the era of nonmonetary and ersatz banking systems. Chapter 3 encompasses 1996–1997, which saw the slow emergence of a monetary regime but during which real commercial banks failed to develop. Chapter 4 looks at 1998 and beyond, offers some ideas about how to convert Russia's ersatz banks into true banks, and assesses the prospects for Russia's financial system if the current system remains in place.

CHAPTER ONE

Russian
Economic Conditions

RUSSIAN PRODUCTIVE POTENTIAL

Since its establishment as a separate state in 1991, Russia's economic performance has been vastly below its productive potential. Per capita income stands at about $4,200 in world market prices, which is lower than the world average of $5,200 and less than one-sixth that of the United States.[1] Per capita income in Russia falls beneath that in Tunisia, Algeria, Botswana, Costa Rica, Colombia, Panama, Brazil, Mexico, and other economies, all of which, at least in the popular image, are relatively poor countries. In Russia, which is the landlord of a space station for American astronauts, something is amiss.

What separates Russia from these other third world countries is its enormous, immediate, current growth potential. Russian income is three, perhaps as much as four, times lower than it could and should be.

First, Russia has the productive capacity in place to double its

---

1. Updated from the World Bank, *World Development Report 1997: The State in a Changing World* (New York: Oxford University Press, 1997), Statistical Appendix, p. 7.

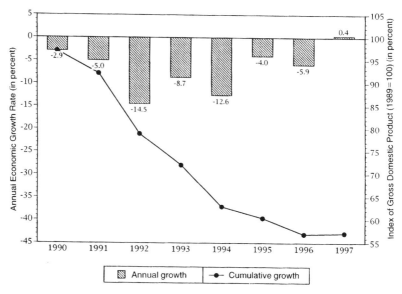

Figure 1. Economic Contraction in Russia, 1990–1997
Source: Russian State Committee on Statistics, regular releases

output of goods and services (its gross domestic product, or GDP). Indeed, just nine years ago, Russian GDP was nearly double current levels. By official and international counts, the economy contracted by 43 percent during 1990–1997 (see figure 1). This accounting may exaggerate the decline in output, as many firms underreported production to reduce their tax liabilities. Offsetting this potential undercounting, however, is the gain that accrued, equivalent to 15 percent of Russian GDP during 1992–1997, when Russia terminated $58 billion in annual energy subsidies to Eastern Europe and the former Soviet Union.[2]

Second, even before the great contraction of the 1990s, Russian industrial investment allowed for a much higher level of output than that produced under the country's faulty, inefficient,

2. The World Bank, *World Development Report 1996: From Plan to Market* (New York: Oxford University Press, 1966), p. 27.

socialist economic arrangements. Western estimates show that the Russian level of capital stock per worker should have produced some 44–52 percent more goods and services than it did.[3]

Third, Russia has a highly educated workforce. Western estimates imply that countries with the same number of years of education per employee as Russia enjoyed in the late 1980s had about 35 percent higher income per capita.[4]

Fourth, and perhaps most important, Russian industry produced, and continues to produce, a large amount of *negative value added* as a result of the application of arbitrary, artificial, distorted, subsidized, and cross-subsidized prices that determine the real cost of production inputs. In other words, a dollar's worth of raw ingredients emerges from the production process as finished merchandise worth less than a dollar. In 1994, the middle year of Russian reforms, Russian industry subtracted 34 percent from the global market value of natural resources alone, without accounting for subtracting the additional value from the intermediate goods used in their production.[5] The mere introduction of true market prices, coupled with the elimination of subsidies, cross-subsidies, cross-debts, and other distortions, would eliminate negative value added in production. The whole country would be better off if the workers in these value-subtracting enterprises were paid full wages to stay at home until sufficient reforms were put in place to add value to production.

---

3. Abram Bergson, "The Communist Efficiency Gap: Alternative Measures," *Comparative Economic Studies* 36, no. 1 (spring 1994): 1–12.

4. Calculated from Robert E. Hall and Chad I. Jones, "The Productivity of Nations," National Bureau of Economic Research, working paper no. 5812, Cambridge, Massachusetts, 1996, p. 45.

5. Calculated from the Russian State Committee on Statistics, *Rossiiskii Statisticheskii Ezhegodnik 1996* (Moscow, 1997), pp. 293–94; world market prices are from the U.S. Bureau of the Census, *Statistical Abstract of the United States 1996* (Washington, D.C.: U.S. Government Printing Office, 1996), pp. 694–97.

By itself, the cessation of value-subtracting economic activities would substantially increase GDP, without any additional investment or other effort.

Taking all four factors together, a three- to fourfold increase is a ballpark estimate of Russia's real productive potential under true private markets in the near term. To this can be added the potential gains from the application of recent Western technological advances to the exploitation of Russia's vast untapped natural resources, assuming that Russian politics can tolerate a much larger role for foreign enterprises.

THE INSTITUTIONAL LEGACIES OF SOCIALISM

A key factor in Russia's failure to develop real banks has been the institutional legacies of socialism. Long decades of socialist rule resulted in deep and pervasive state penetration of the economy and society. Under central planning, the Russian economy was highly centralized, monopolistic, protected from foreign competition and exposure; it was also structurally anomalous. It lacked most of the social, legal, and institutional infrastructure taken for granted even in underdeveloped market economies.

The old Soviet banking system was a monobank system, centered on the state bank, Gosbank, which covered the entire Soviet Union through its many branches and collection systems. All monetary transactions went through Gosbank or one of its affiliated banks. The primary purpose of the banking system was to support the economic system of central planning, in which government bureaucrats allocated inputs (raw materials, labor, investment), outputs (told enterprises what to produce and where to ship goods), set prices and wages, determined incomes, and rationed consumption. The banking system mirrored the real economy by recording financial flows that tracked the flow of goods and by supplying credit to aid plan fulfillment and finance investment. It also supplied cash to enterprises for wages to employees to facilitate daily transactions.

In 1987–1988, during perestroika, a two-tiered banking system was created. The state bank split into three branch state banks for (1) industry, (2) construction and utilities, and (3) agriculture. Private, nominally commercial banks emerged in 1988–1990 and mushroomed thereafter. In 1991, Gosbank became the Central Bank of Russia (CBR), which held responsibility for monetary policy, commercial bank supervision, and facilitating interbank settlements. Other state banks were reformed into joint-stock banks owned by enterprises, government agencies, and government-connected private groups. All these commercial banks, however, remained dependent on subsidized credits from the CBR and, thus, were its de facto branches.

Moreover, in 1992 the government established a secretive body named the Credit-Monetary Commission, chaired by a senior deputy prime minister. The chairman of the Central Bank of Russia was the ranking member of this commission, but he does not exercise the influence and power that Alan Greenspan enjoys at the U.S. Federal Reserve Board. The commission sets targets of monetary expansion and credit for commercial banks, thereby replacing the Politburo of the Communist Party, which had set monetary and credit targets during Soviet times. In practical terms, the Credit-Monetary Commission made an independent central bank impossible, despite the existence of legal statutes that promise autonomy.

The reason the government could not let the CBR be independent is that the commission required individual commercial banks, which sought subsidized credit from the CBR, to allocate that credit to specific enterprises in accordance with commission directives. Once these credit allocation targets were satisfied, banks had some discretion in reselling unallocated central bank credit. As most banks were owned by, or connected to, enterprises, the banks basically serviced their founders or subsidiaries with government money.

From their inception, commercial banks served as government check-cashing windows, similar to those used by U.S. welfare recipients. Banks were inherently insolvent because their loans were not supposed to be recoverable. The commercial banking system of Russia began its existence with inherently bad assets. When these assets were dissipated by inflation, a new stock of bad assets accumulated because of government-directed credit. As a result, banks required either a continuous flow of central bank refinancing at subsidized interest rates or, when this means was eliminated, other forms of government refinancing and recapitalization.

BACKGROUND TO ECONOMIC REFORM

Analyzing the transition economies of Central and Eastern Europe and Asia has created a new area of scholarly inquiry, producing a spate of books and journals exploring a variety of transition issues as these countries try to make the adjustment from their former socialist systems to market economies. It is not clear that the word *transition* is suitable for Russia. A more appropriate concept might take the form of asking what is required to destroy the old economic and financial systems and then, on a clean slate, how to build new systems.

In 1991, there was no broad consensus on the correct transition strategy. Between March 1985 and October 1990, varying teams of economists proposed twelve different economic reform plans to then Soviet leader Mikhail Gorbachev. All twelve were subsequently dismissed or abandoned.

The first genuine reform measure was the first privatization law in 1991, which established the right to private property in productive assets. In 1992, the government liberalized prices and began a small-scale privatization program, followed by a voucher privatization program. A new system of ownership structure was created, but that structure was not private property in a normal sense. The reason, as explained below, is that private property was not accompanied by *private budgets*.

ERSATZ PRIVATIZATION

It is important to dispel the notion that privatization created real private property in Russia. In reality, spontaneous privatization in the former Soviet Union began in 1988 when the Law on Enterprise allowed enterprises to withhold the remittance of profits to the government and convert them into wages and managerial bonuses. Private ownership of previously government-owned enterprises was initially acquired by insiders but not in a form that could be sold or traded. In financial terms, ownership did not take the form of securities in joint-stock corporations, which would entitle holders to a share of the enterprise and a portion of its profits.

The government proceeded with a program of voucher privatization, which segregated the country's assets into two unequal parts. All highly profitable enterprises, especially in natural resources, remained government owned, with a proportion of transferable shares distributed to workers and managers of these firms. All other enterprises were converted into joint-stock corporations, or securitized, and their shares were exchangeable for broadly distributed vouchers (every Russian citizen received a voucher).

Between October 1992 and June 1995, a process of spontaneous privatization and voucher distribution and use resulted in the sale of more than fifteen thousand large state-owned enterprises (more than 118,000 for the whole economy). By mid-1995, 75.5 percent of all industrial firms were nominally private, producing 87.7 percent of industrial output and employing 77.7 percent of industrial workers (more than 18 million people).

Most Russian citizens placed their vouchers in largely unregulated voucher investment funds and became shareholders of those mutual funds. The investment privatization funds, IPFs as they became known in many transition economies, exchanged the vouchers they collected from individuals for shares of enterprises slated for voucher privatization. Most of the funds then vanished. Individual Russians were hard-pressed to identify what they owned and rarely received any dividends. In 1996, the government considered closing and banning the remaining voucher investment funds because of widespread fraud and the impossibility of monitoring and supervising them. Still, some funds remain. Where and with whom the actual stock of voucher-privatized enterprises ended up remains a mystery because there is no property registry. Scores of holding companies own other holding companies, which own enterprise shares. Invisible and illegitimate ownership created further incentives to run down assets rather than foster new investment.

In 1995, the government began to sell through various, largely rigged cash auctions the truly valuable assets that were spared the voucher episode of privatization. The first wave of these sales was best known as "loans for shares." To justify the subsidized transfer of highly profitable assets in natural resource firms to a small group of selected banks, the government gave the banks shares in "temporary trust" for state-owned resource firms in exchange for their loans to the budget. Banks financed those loans from government deposits they held (a bizarre circular process). When the government failed to repay the loans (as expected), the elite banks became owners of a large chunk of Russian natural resources. (See chapter 3 for details and unforeseen consequences.)

Revenues from privatization fell from 0.28 percent of GDP in 1995 to 0.11 percent in 1996. Activity picked up in January 1997 with the sale of an 8.5 percent stake in United Energy Systems. In the third quarter, the government sold a 25 percent stake plus one share in Svyazinvest, the telecommunications holding company, which raised almost half as much revenue as all previous privatizations combined.[6] The government also sold major stakes in Tyumen Oil Company and Norilsk Nickel; each of those sales was managed and won respectively by the insider banks that had advanced the loans for those shares (financed by government deposits at these banks) in the first place.

Today, almost all production is nominally in private hands, and few industrial workers remain state employees. But this does not mean that the Russian economy is built on a foundation of private property or that private enterprises are really private. On the contrary. *What appear to be private firms are not really private because they share a common budget with the public sector.* So-called private firms and private banks in Russia have served largely as appendages to a differently constructed system of state control and financing than was the case in the former socialist system. The lines between the public and the nominally private sectors are so blurred that government financing of economic activity has been far in excess of the ostensible 30 percent ratio that defines government expenditures as a share of GDP, rendering this measure almost meaningless.

The evidence for the proposition that the size of the government exceeds 30 percent of GDP is the large share of the negative

6. The sale of a 25 percent stake in Svyazinvest was the first large-scale privatization that appeared to be conducted at a real competitive auction. In that vein, it was probably the first real market privatization, rather than a preferential giveaway of state assets.

value added in production previously mentioned. In a privately financed economy, firms cannot produce negative value added (output whose market value is less than that of its material resource inputs) for long. Such firms and industries soon go broke. Russia is different. One-third of the value of natural resources and one-half of the final value added of industrial output amounts to value subtraction, a process that survives on the basis of subsidies from the natural resource sector and the few profitable firms in other sectors. Neither income nor expenses derived from production are truly private. All flows of funds are linked to a regime of subsidies and cross-subsidies, which creates a common budget for all the ostensibly separate entities. The common budget is facilitated through the interplay of the government and the banking system. Within this system, the appearance of domestic free market prices is deceptive. All prices embody subsidies and taxes in one form or another. Prices serve a fiscal, not a market role, as is always the case under socialism.

The normal meaning of private property rights is exclusive ownership of assets and their returns. So-called private assets that do not generate real private returns are private in name only. When these so-called private assets generate income, largely on the basis of access to government subsidies, they are of little long-term value to their new owners, who face incentives (given the insecurity of their property rights in these assets) to strip them of their real economic value. The value that remains, after real assets have been stripped, is the claims that the owners make on the real resources of other enterprises and actors (by accumulating debts to other enterprises, banks, and the tax authorities they cannot pay or do not expect to pay). Such a system perversely transforms liabilities into assets.

Russian-style privatization, which has thus far amounted to continuous access to government subsidies, is the antithesis of real privatization. A famous theorem in economics, named after

Nobel laureate Ronald H. Coase, states that, regardless of initial ownership, real tradeable private assets will ultimately end up in the hands of the most efficient owners, who will bid them away from their initial owners in the expectation of securing higher returns.[7]

The corollary for Russia is that it does not matter if privatization was conducted through vouchers, private placement, or other means or who were the initial owners. The most capable extractors of government subsidies will eventually bid away property rights through money, force, or government connivance. In the upside-down Coase world of Russia, private property ultimately ended up in the hands of the most capable predators of public income, not in the hands of those who might use it to generate the highest possible economic return. Nominal privatization transformed explicit socialism into quasi socialism. The big financial-industrial groups, having an appearance of privateness, simply merged with the central government as the owners and allocators of national resources. The process of privatization in Russia turned out to be counterproductive and explains why it failed to generate growth. It also highlights the need to achieve real privatization, which requires separation of public and private budgets. No one should be deceived into thinking that these FIGs, as financial-industrial groups are known, are real private enterprises that sink or swim on their own.

DATA ON RUSSIA

Goskomstat (the State Statistical Committee) has had to create a system of "real" national income accounts that reflect the new economic realities of Russia. This is easier said than done, and

---

7. Ronald H. Coase, "The Problem of Social Cost," *Journal of Law and Economics* 3, no. 3 (October 1960): 1–44.

the organization still has a long way to go. Socialist statistical systems did not have a Western system of national income accounts or the concepts of gross domestic (or gross national) product and national income. They counted only physical output, not value added and not services. The true problem is prices, which were not, and still are not, real market prices. It is hard, therefore, to subtract intermediate inputs and find the final value added. Also, changing estimates of the shadow economy arbitrarily distort the data on GDP and growth, making it hard to count and quantify new firms. The introduction of an explicit tax system (which replaced the old system of enterprises turning over their income to the state) encourages firms to understate output and profit. The output of small firms and providers of services tends to be undercounted. By contrast, as previously mentioned, the contraction of output may be underestimated because the value of exported natural resources increased when Russia phased out energy subsidies to Eastern Europe and the former Soviet Union. This unrecorded addition to GDP, about 15 percent over the 1990s, hides an equivalent contraction of real output. Despite its shortcomings, the State Statistical Committee still remains the primary source of raw data on the Russian economy.

Some State Statistical Committee data are reproduced in English in *Russian Economic Trends*, a publication of the London School of Economics (with the cooperation of the Russian government), financed by the European Commission's technical assistance program (TACIS). A monthly update of *Russian Economic Trends* is published with a few week's delay and is available on the World Wide Web. The data encompass such standard indicators as inflation, the budget, money supply, the foreign exchange market, financial markets, foreign trade, output and investment, consumption and wages, and unemployment.

The International Monetary Fund, World Bank, Organization for Economic Cooperation and Development (OECD), European

Bank for Reconstruction and Development (EBRD), and a number of commercial banks routinely publish assessments of the Russian economy. The CBR publishes a variety of statistical bulletins and pamphlets. It also maintains a summary data series on the Web, both in English and in Russian.

Three problems plague Russian data: consistency over time, consistency between sources, and general reliability. Every two or three years, the CBR significantly changes its definitions, measurements, and subsequent numbers on such basic matters as money, credit, good and bad banking assets, deposits, and banks' equity capital. Periodically, the health of the banking system is suddenly uplifted by abrupt statistical changes, which makes creating consistent historial series both difficult and suspect. The data on money and banking variables reported by the CBR and the State Statistical Committee do not match, with no obvious tendency. Our numerous inquiries to the leadership of the Central Bank, the State Statistical Committee, the Ministry of Finance, and the government about specific data changes, definitions, and mismatches revealed more uncertainty than clarity. The worst problem, however, is the outright falsification of the balance sheets of the banking system and major banks.

According to a published statement by the chairman of one of the largest Russian commercial banks, Inkombank, the CBR and the commercial banks reached an unwritten agreement in 1997 to use creative accounting in designing their balance sheets to hide sunk losses, which may wipe out the entire equity of major banks. The specific methods of this accounting convention remain secret.[8] The fraudulent construction of bank balance sheets is sanctioned to boost their creditworthiness. Private Western accounting firms are familiar with this problem; their typical

---

8. Vladimir Vinogradov, "Any Banker Is a Very Lonely Man," *Nezavisimaia Gazeta* (Moscow), December 25, 1997, p. 4.

published audits of major Russian banks contain a disclaimer that the audit is based on the data provided by the client and that the auditor is not responsible for the final numbers in the balance sheet.[9]

A huge academic literature (books and journal articles) has materialized on Russia. Most of that work focuses on personalities and various reform topics (e.g., privatization, price liberalization, political intrigue). That literature is highly contentious in that the proponents of the many reform plans put forth since 1985 try to defend their particular recommendations. There is a struggle for turf among the contending academic factions that had (or want) the ears of the Russian government. As a result, much of the literature is self-serving. Fortunately for our work, we can draw for insight and comparative analysis on an excellent transition literature not specifically devoted to Russia.[10]

9. Foreign accounting companies and auditors routinely disclaim responsibility for the integrity of the data in their published reports that set forth balance sheets and profit and loss statements of Russian banks. See, for example, Arthur Andersen's published audit of Bank Menatep in *Finansovye Izvestiia*, no. 95 (December 1, 1995): 3.

10. See Erik Berglof and Gerard Roland, "Bank Restructuring and Soft Budget Constraints in Financial Transition, *Journal of the Japanese and International Economies* 9, no. 4 (December 1995): 354–75; Enrico C. Perotti, "A Taxonomy of Post-Socialist Financial Systems: Decentralized Enforcement and the Creation of Inside Money," *Economics of Transition* 2, no. 1 (January 1994): 71–81; Enrico C. Perotti, "Bank Lending in Transition Economies," *Journal of Banking and Finance* 17, no. 5 (September 1993): 1021–32; Guillermo A. Calvo and Fabrizio Coricelli, "Inter-Enterprise Arrears in Economies in Transition," in Robert Holzmann, Janos Gacs, and George Winckler, eds., *Output Decline in Eastern Europe: Unavoidable, External Influence or Homemade?* (Dordrecht, Boston, and London: Kluwer Academic Publishers, 1995), pp. 193–212; Guillermo A. Calvo and Fabrizio Coricelli, "Credit Market Imperfections and Output Response in Previously Centrally Planned Economies," in Gerard Caprio, David Folkerts-Landau, and Timothy D. Lane, eds., *Building Sound Finance in Emerging Market Economies* (Washington, D.C.: The International Monetary Fund and the World Bank, 1994), pp. 257–94; Steve H. Hanke, Lars Jonung, and Kurt Schuler, *Russian Currency and Finance: A Currency Board Approach to Reform* (London and New York: Routledge, 1993);

Ronald I. McKinnon, *The Order of Economic Liberalization: Financial Control in the Transition to a Market Economy*, 2d edition (Baltimore and London: Johns Hopkins University Press, 1993); Guillermo A. Calvo and Manmohan S. Kumar, "Money Demand, Bank Credit, and Economic Performance in Former Socialist Economies," *IMF Staff Papers* 41, no. 2 (June 1994): 314–49; and Ronald I. McKinnon, "Financial Growth and Macroeconomic Stability in China, 1978–1992: Implications for Russia and other Transitional Economies," *Journal of Comparative Economics* 18, no. 3 (1994): 438–70.

CHAPTER TWO

The Nonmonetary System and the Ersatz Banking System in Russia: 1991–1995

In 1991, the newly independent Russian Federation was rich in assets, including a highly educated population, world-class science, a large pool of private savings and deposits, a generally high savings rate, great entrepreneurial drive, widespread infrastructure (even if substandard by Western comparisons), and vast natural resources. The new Russian Federation inherited $69 billion of foreign debt from the Soviet period, a manageable level given the size, resources, and export earnings of the new country. The new government, in principle, was committed to the process of economic reform and received generous intellectual support from the West from a raft of institutional and individual economic advisers. On paper, the prospects for growth were encouraging.

By 1995, chronic inflation totaled 200,000 percent and a protracted decline approached 40 percent of national income and consumption. Between 1991 and 1995, the official gross domestic product (GDP) contracted (negative growth) every year and every quarter (see figures 1 and 2). Industrial production also fell every quarter during 1992–1995. Although the spontaneous privatization and monetary instability engendered by the 1988

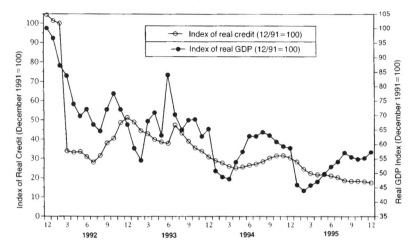

Figure 2. Indexes of Real Credit and Real Gross Domestic Product, Russia, 1992–1995. Real credit represents commercial bank credits to enterprises at the end of the month, two months before, in constant December 1991 rubles, deflated by the consumer price index and indexed to December 1991. To allow for the GDP lag, the credit data precede the GDP data by two months. Monthly GDP values are deflated by the consumer price index (CPI) and adjusted for the difference between the CPI and the GDP deflator in 1992. The GDP data for 1992 are reconstituted from the industrial production series.
Source: Russian State Committee on Statistics and Central Bank of Russia, various releases.

enterprise reform generated a mild contraction during 1990–1991, the big reform of January 1992 was the direct source of accelerated contraction and extreme inflation.

A review of the Russian economy during 1991–1995 indicates that Russia failed to develop effective monetary and banking systems. A more accurate way of stating the problem is to say that Russia had a *nonsystem of monetary control* and regulation and a *nonbanking system*, or a *system of ersatz banks*. Until viable monetary and banking systems are established, the Russian economy will continue to flounder.

AN OVERVIEW OF RUSSIA'S
MONETARY NONSYSTEM: 1991–1995

One principal role of a commercial banking system in normal economies is to uphold the independence of the monetary system. An independent monetary system normally focuses on tasks of monetary management (see below); it stays scrupulously away from the direct or indirect financing of production, which is left to commercial banks. When monetary systems are used to finance production, however, they become a means for conducting industrial policy and attaining specific production targets. History shows that using monetary systems in this way, a hallmark of socialist economies, typically results in high inflation and poor economic performance.

Under central planning, money served primarily as an accounting device to monitor and enforce production quotas of inputs and outputs. The government set prices according to the planners' preferences, with consideration of the pressures facing enterprise managers. At any set of prices and specified quantities of inputs and outputs, an enterprise that ended a quarter or a year with positive money balances was considered to be achieving or even outperforming its plan target. The government then took back any excess money balances, as it was the rightful owner of the residual income.

Any enterprise that ended the quarter or the year with negative money balances was presumed to have overspent its quota of inputs (for example, used too much labor or diverted its output to internal use) or underproduced more valuable outputs. In these instances, the government might discipline enterprise managers or use other means to enforce production targets. Regardless of what other corrective measures might be employed to reach plan targets, the net effect of using the monetary system in this way was that the government inevitably accommodated with newly printed money all excess production, even if useless and wasteful, and all enterprise losses. The alternative was to close down money-losing enterprises, but this only made it more difficult to meet plan targets. The system led to an inherently loose monetary policy.[1]

Monetary policy under central planning was jointly determined by the government and enterprises—this is the essence of the socialist fiscal system under central planning. Strict enforcement of production quotas, remittance of enterprise money balances, and wage controls were necessary to prevent a monetary explosion and intolerable shortages. Potential inflation was repressed. When the Soviet government stopped requiring enterprises to remit profits (after the Enterprise Law came into force in 1988), enterprises converted their profits into higher wages and managerial bonuses. The socialist monetary system automatically accommodated this conversion. As would be expected, the flood of new money quickly devalued the currency in terms of goods, resulting in high inflation, partly open, partly repressed. Enterprises stopped shipping goods for money and switched to barter. Shortages mounted. Constituent republics took over state bank branches and inflated the currency quickly in the race for goods that remained in the trading system. The monetary system of the Soviet Union collapsed in late 1990–1991; the Soviet Union itself dissolved in late 1991.

A market economy requires a monetary system independent from the financing of production, which is the exact opposite of the Soviet system of central planning. But an independent monetary system alone is not sufficient. A market economy also requires a commercial banking system (and capital markets), es-

1. Janos Kornai, "Resource-Constrained Versus Demand-Constrained Systems," *Econometrica* 47, no. 4 (July 1979): 801–19, and Kornai, "The Soft Budget Constraint," *Kyklos* 39, no. 1 (spring 1986): 3–30.

pecially in transition economies. A real monetary system and real commercial banks, separately yet in combination, provide the conditions to finance production, which the monetary system alone provided under central planning. *It is not enough just to rename the state bank a central bank and establish private payment franchises and call them commercial banks.*

The role of money in transition economies must be recast from its previous accounting function under central planning to a medium of private exchange and a store of private value. Without money, people cannot retain and store income. Without income, people would not voluntarily produce beyond subsistence (and we would be back to the forced production of central planning). Money is at the origin of private productive incentives and economic growth.

Let us summarize the transformation of money from central planning to the market economy and its importance in laying a foundation for growth in transition economies: The switch from central planning to a market economy means that the monetary system, which financed production, must become independent of production. Money, instead of accommodating production, must become the medium of exchange. Money instead of an accounting device for monitoring and enforcing production must become a unit of account in trade. Household savings under central planning, in effect owned jointly with the government and subject to confiscation and forced borrowing, must become a store of private value. Money must change from a vehicle to redistribute goods, services, and incomes and become an embodiment of private incomes and expenses.

The primary purpose of a monetary system in normal market economies is to ensure a stable currency for the dual purpose of facilitating economic transactions and providing a store of private value, which creates conditions and incentives for economic growth. In pursuit of these objectives, the typical normal monetary institution issues currency to finance daily transactions, supplies liquidity to the economy, regulates the growth of credit, strives for price stability, regulates banks, determines some means of linking internal prices with external prices (through some exchange-rate regime), and, if the monetary and fiscal systems are linked (as they are in most contemporary economies), manages the portfolio of government debt. In normal circumstances, that is, in normal countries with normal central banks or central monetary authorities, those tasks are executed with varying degrees of success. The central bank/monetary authorities issue high-powered base money (notes and coins), conduct open market operations with government securities, require commercial banks to maintain reserves with the central monetary authorities, set short-term interest rates, regulate banks, choose an exchange-rate regime, and so on.

Most central monetary authorities are guided by explicit or implicit rules that emphasize one or more objectives and require one or more tools of policy. The normal chief objective is to maintain price stability but with an attendant concern for growth. The normal tools of monetary policy are three: (1) targeting some monetary growth indicator, typically M_2 (currency, demand deposits, time deposits), (2) setting interest rates, or (3) maintaining some kind of fixed or quasi-fixed exchange-rate regime. Once any of the three tools are put in place, the others adjust more or less automatically. Some large industrial countries follow a heterodox policy of fine-tuning among two or all three tools of monetary policy, sometimes raising or lowering interest rates, sometimes increasing or decreasing monetary targets, and sometimes revaluing or devaluing the national currency, while keeping a watchful eye on the other two.

Russia's monetary system during 1991–1995 is best described as a nonsystem. During 1991–1995, the CBR was unable to control the supply of money, the price level, or the exchange rate.

It was unable to prevent a collapse of the ruble. It failed to regulate commercial banks effectively. Perhaps worst of all, it was unable and unwilling to protect the store of private value entrusted to it, namely, households' deposits in the government-owned Savings Bank.

A normal monetary system begins with high-powered base money, which consists of notes and coins in circulation and reserves held by commercial banks with the central monetary authorities (and, in some instances, net foreign reserves held by the central monetary authorities). Starting with high-powered base money, banks accept demand and time deposits, which provide the resources for lending. (Banks are in business to make money. Normal banks in normal countries do so by lending out depositors' funds at a profit.) The standard money multiplier effect converts high-powered base money into a much larger credit structure. In mature credit systems, the demand deposit–to-cash ratio ranges between 3–4 to 1. The broader M_2 measure of demand plus time deposits–to-cash ratio typically exceeds 10 to 1.

During 1991–1995, the Russian nonsystem was a fiat monetary system with a vengeance. By the end of 1995, the monetary base consisted of 80.8 trillion rubles in cash (about $17 billion at the exchange rate of the day), supported by about $6 billion in net international reserves. Russian households held about $37 billion in U.S. currency, but these banknotes were not part of the official money supply or the country's formal credit structure. The high level of dollar savings, amounting to 15–20 percent of household income, was well in excess of ruble savings (see figure 3). Apart from cash in circulation, Russia lacked a mature system of ruble demand and time deposits, a consequence of chronic inflation and the loss of confidence in the banking system after the loss of deposits.

Since 1992, ruble deposits have ranged between 3 and 8 percent of household income. The savings rate remained high during

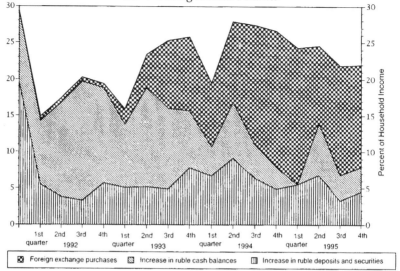

Figure 3. Russian Household Savings in Rubles and Foreign Exchange, 1991–1995 (in percent of total household income).
Source: Central Bank of Russia and Russian State Committee on Statistics, various releases.

1992–1995, exceeding 20 percent of household income (see figure 3). The composition of savings, however, changed dramatically. Beginning in 1992, households began to substitute ruble cash for ruble deposits and then, during 1993–1995, substituted dollars for rubles. This can be described as a process of debanking and dollarization.

In practice, the CBR did not specify a program of money creation that it then faithfully attempted to follow. Rather, money (cash, CBR credit) was issued in response to debt created either by the government through its budget deficit (including the combined budget deficits of the eighty-nine regional governments—collectively, the regional budgets are almost as large as the federal budget and their deficits are larger) or, more important, by the credit enterprises extended to one another in exchange for goods and services. Interenterprise credit, however, is not normal trade credit (given by one firm to another as in a normal economy), which is based on creditworthiness and never continuously extended if not repaid.

Between 1991 and 1995, Russia failed to achieve monetary stability, either in terms of a stable currency or in terms of a consistent, single-digit inflation. In 1991, the last year of the Soviet Union, the midyear exchange rate of the Russian ruble was R42 to $1. It subsequently fell from R180:$1 in January 1992 to R4,640:$1 at the end of 1995, a staggering loss in value. During 1995, the inflation rate was 131.3 percent (CPI), although this was something of an improvement from 839.9 percent in 1993.

The chief cause of Russia's failure to develop an effective monetary system is found in the problem of enterprise arrears, which was the driving force in fiscal and monetary policy during this period.

Enterprise Arrears

In January 1992, the government decontrolled input and output flows, prices, and wages. Enterprises immediately took to financing one another through an enormous surge in interenterprise credit, opening virtually unlimited lines of credit to one another. Enterprise credits approached half of GDP. The creation of credits among enterprises during 1992–1995 far exceeded total bank credit and the entire ruble money stock (see figure 4). When the bills came due and enterprises could not pay, the government and the central bank stepped in to allocate funds to indebted enterprises. In so doing, the government transformed bad lines of credit into good ones. This covering of bad debts further encouraged enterprises to extend more credit to one another, and the process repeated. The creation of enterprise credit thus became the driving engine of fiscal and monetary policy.

During 1992–1995 this strange driving force of monetary policy operated as follows. Credit (interenterprise credit) was given

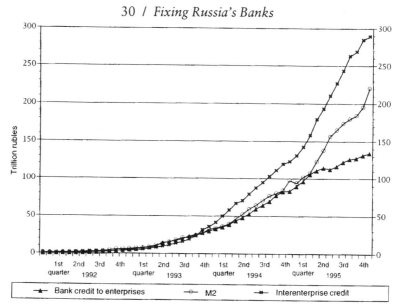

Figure 4. Interenterprise Credit, Bank Credit, and the Money Stock, Russia, 1992–1995.
Sources: Money and bank credit: Russian Central Bank, various releases. Interenterprise credit: Russian State Committee on Statistics, various releases.

by one firm to another with little or no regard for the other firm's willingness or ability to pay. The failure to pay bills by enterprises resulted in a massive accumulation of interenterprise debt (also called enterprise arrears, or EAs). It amounted to a backlog of delinquent accounts payable on the debtor side and unrecoverable (uncollected or uncollectible) accounts receivable on the creditor side. These delinquent and unrecoverable bills simply piled up. Some bills were paid, but new, larger bills were incurred; and the entire system expanded as it accumulated more and more bad debt. Thus it is important to look at the total amount of EAs as they increased, rather than at the share of EAs that were legally overdue at any point in time.

In terms of monthly GDP, the stock of unpaid receivables increased from 119 percent in January 1993 to 131 percent in

January 1994 to 157 percent in January 1995 and to 185 percent in January 1996. At the end of 1995, the stock of EAs equaled R289.3 trillion ($62.4 billion).

Enterprise arrears to the government (including the federal government), as well as pensions and other trust funds of federal social programs financed by payroll taxes and regional governments, rose in tandem, reaching R86.8 trillion ($18.6 billion) at the end of 1995. Delinquent enterprise payments on bank loans amounted to R37.7 trillion. Although that number may seem small, it represents 22.9 percent of total loans because total bank credits to enterprises are modest. Recall that, according to international standards, 6–8 percent of nonperforming loans in a loan portfolio is considered problematic. When the share of nonperforming loans exceeds 10 percent, it is regarded as a crisis and a sign of structural insolvency of the banking system.

At the end of 1995, M_2 was equivalent to about 13.3 percent of GDP and the broadest definition of money was equivalent to 17.5 percent of GDP. The stock of unrecoverable enterprise receivables was 31 percent higher than M_2 and, at R289.3 trillion ($62.4 billion), was exactly equal to the broad money supply. In effect, interenterprise credit became and remained the principal determinant of the domestic money supply.

Almost every creditor is also a debtor, thereby resulting in a cobweb of mutual indebtedness. One consequence of EAs is late payment of wages to workers: Wage arrears rose from a low 7 percent of the monthly wage bill in the first quarter of 1993 to 46 percent in mid-1994 to about 80 percent at the end of 1995. Since enterprises must pay salaries at some point, they required some source of money, which was the public purse: CBR credits and government-subsidized bonds or currency or both. Enterprises created accounting money, which was transformed into government debt and explicit money. They did so through EAs, the equivalent of a quasi-fiscal government deficit, which was ultimately monetized into real money. It is as if each of the fifty thousand important enterprises in Russia were a branch of the federal Ministry of Finance and, because of subsequent monetization, also a branch of the CBR but with a time lag.

Despite price liberalization and privatization, the government continued to allocate money to enterprises. The government could no longer borrow from households, having wiped out their savings through inflation and highly negative interest rates in 1992. Nor could the government tap into new household savings because the public had lost confidence in it. Its only resort, in those circumstances, was to create new money to underwrite budget deficits. The Russian government and the Central Bank became the lenders of first, not last, resort. Enterprise arrears became synonymous with (implicit) government debt awaiting monetization.

CBR or government issue of cash, credits, or subsidized bonds validated the (implicit) state debt created among enterprises. *Validation of enterprise debt by the government had the fiscal effect of perpetuating the inherited common budget, a single credit card, for the entire economy, public and private.* As in the old regime, individual enterprises, regardless of whether they remained state owned or became private, did not face the private budget constraint of most private firms in normal economies. Enterprises extended credits to one another, raised prices, and accumulated mutual debts. In so doing, they compelled the government to monetize these debts through a number of fiscal and monetary tools used by the CBR and Ministry of Finance, a process far removed from any market

With the collapse of real credit after 1992 (see figure 2), Russian firms lived off debt and government monetization of that debt during 1992–1995, which periodically reduced the stock of EAs. The real and financial sectors of the Russian economy were on a treadmill: Increases in money supply covered past debts, rolled over existing credits, and invited the accumulation of new debts and the issue of new credits.

The accommodation of EAs by the central bank naturally led to a rapid increase in money, which inflated the currency and depreciated the ruble. Russia was hit with a double whammy— rising prices and economic contraction.

The monetary regime in effect during 1991–1995 amounted to the absence of a monetary system because the monetary authority was unable to control the money supply over any sustained period of time. Almost every firm in this nonsystem was empowered to write postdated government checks.

The defining characteristic of Russia's monetary nonsystem during 1991–1995 was the absence of a firm separation of enterprises (private, joint stock, state owned) from the public purse. It is as if the government and private enterprises shared the same account number for all financial transactions. The fact that the share of industrial workers in "privatized" enterprises had risen from 1 percent in January 1992 to 82 percent by mid-1994 does not mean that these enterprises were truly private—by definition, if a private firm cannot make ends meet, it goes out of business. Rather, the financial budget of the country's balance sheet combining the public and private sectors, taken as a whole, amounted to a *common budget*.

During 1992–1995, monetization of EAs (enterprise budget deficits) was the main source of inflation in Russia—more than 200,000 percent by 1995. It also caused a massive depreciation of the ruble, which declined from an exchange rate of $1 = R42 in mid-1991 to surpass $1 = R4,640 in December 1995. (In 1992, as part of the price liberalization reforms, the exchange-rate regime was liberalized from its Soviet-era, rigidly fixed exchange rate.) From time to time, the CBR tightened credit in an attempt to fight inflation. But tight credit, given the overhang of EAs and the threat of widespread bankruptcies, which threatened the destruction of the country's tax base, invariably forced the CBR to relax its credit and money policies. It was thus unable to break the inflationary cycle.

COMMERCIAL BANKS IN RUSSIA: THE ABSENCE OF NORMAL BANKS DURING 1991–1995

The main theme of this volume is that commercial banks in Russia were not, and still are not, normal banks as found in market economies. They do not accept deposits paying a market rate of interest or make loans on the basis of commercial criteria. They do not fulfill the normal role of intermediating household deposits to enterprises, thereby converting savings into investment. Instead, Russian banks have served primarily as government agencies that redistribute public funds to enterprises, mostly to favored ones, or as profit centers trading in foreign exchange, government bonds, or insider lending. The banks may look and feel as though they are private enterprises, especially to outsiders, but in fact they have largely served the government's discretionary allocation of subsidies to other enterprises and also financed political causes.

In 1995, Russia had more than 2,500 banks apart from the state-owned Savings Bank. To quantify their liabilities, at the end of 1995, they held household deposits worth $5.2 billion at the prevailing exchange rate, an astonishingly meager 1.5 percent of GDP and only about 11 percent of the value of outstanding rubles. Even combined with the Savings Bank, all household deposits only constituted 4.3 percent of GDP. On their books, the banks held enterprise debt with a book value of $26 billion (about one-third of which was nonperforming), a mere 7 percent of GDP. Total credit (including the Savings Bank) represented 8.1 percent of GDP. The total of enterprise and government demand deposits held with commercial banks, along with household deposits held with the giant Savings Bank, amounted to total credit resources of 11.7 percent in rubles and dollars (only 8.4 percent in rubles) of Russian GDP. As to assets, the banks held home mortgages and other household debt in the neighborhood of $270 million, an almost invisible 0.08 percent of GDP (compared with U.S. financial institutions with $4.6 trillion, or 70 percent of U.S. GDP). The rest of their assets consisted of claims on the government and enterprises on their common account. Figure 5 shows the collapse in deposits and bank credit during 1992–1995.

Overall, the Russian banking system was structurally insolvent in 1995, with nonperforming debt constituting about one-third

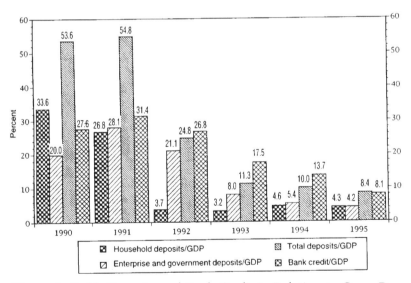

Figure 5. Ruble Deposits and Bank Credit in Relation to Gross Domestic Product, Russia, 1990–1995. Ruble deposits and credits only. The data on foreign exchange deposits and credit were not available before 1996.
Sources: Bank credits and deposits: Central Bank of Russia and Russian State Committee on Statistics, various releases. GDP: Russian State Committee on Statistics, various releases.

of all ruble loans and one-quarter of total loans (see figure 6). The banking system avoided collapse through periodic government bailouts (aided by foreign grants and loans).

Origins of Russia's Commercial Banks

To understand the problem of creating real banks and credit markets in Russia, a few words are required on how banks were initially established after the state bank, Gosbank, was dismantled. By the early 1990s, three types of banks had developed: joint-venture banks (e.g., Dialog Bank), domestic commercial banks, and "wildcat" banks. Wildcat banks were those formed by enterprises, industrial sectors, and local governments. They grew rapidly to constitute the majority of all banks (in number, not in assets) because capital requirements were low and regulation was virtually nonexistent. Their main activity was to borrow from the CBR at subsidized rates and lend the proceeds to designated enterprises, which were the legal or de facto owners of the banks (firms established their own banks). Most of the assets of the Russian banking system are held by the large domestic commercial banks (e.g., Inkombank, Uneximbank), which provide short-term credit to enterprises but derive the bulk of their income from foreign currency trading, dealing in government bonds, and other nonlending activities.

On January 1, 1996, Russia had 2,598 commercial banks with 5,580 branch offices, in addition to state-owned giants such as the Savings Bank, the Bank for Foreign Economic Relations (Vneshekonombank), and the Bank for Foreign Trade (Vneshtorgbank). Although most banks are registered as private corporations, in reality the federal government owned large stakes in major Moscow banks (e.g., Menatep, National Credit, etc.), while regional and municipal governments owned large stakes in the leading banks in their cities. The rest of the shares usually

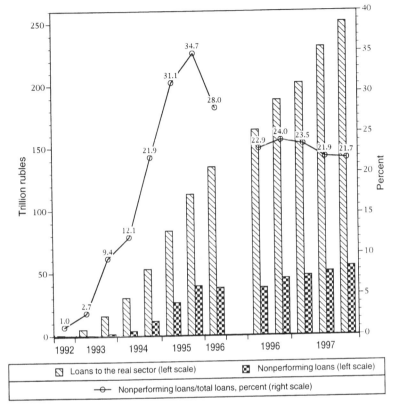

Figure 6. Credit and Nonperforming Loans in the Russian Banking Sector, 1992–1997. Before and on January 1996, total credit and nonperforming loans are in rubles only. After January 1996, total and nonperforming loans include both ruble and foreign exchange denominated contracts.
Source: Central Bank of Russia, various releases.

belonged to state-owned enterprises and large corporations where the government also held a sizable or controlling interest or subsidized them.

The system of enterprise ownership of banks took the German model, in which banks hold substantial stakes in leading firms, to an extreme. The Russian firms owned their banks outright and were the principal borrowers of funds from the banks they owned, giving new meaning to concept of "insider" lending. It worked because the government underwrote the implicit debt created by enterprise banks making (bad or risky) loans to themselves. The financial effect was that commercial banks transformed good liabilities (deposits) into bad assets (loans to their owners). They survived thanks to CBR and government subsidies, which allowed them to roll over and perpetuate bad credit.

Decline of Real Credit

As previously documented, the collapse of credit in Russia is almost unparalleled in modern history. Between 1991 and 1995, credit resources to the Russian economy contracted by about 80 percent. Using constant December 1991 prices, real credit declined from R439.4 billion (credit granted solely in rubles) at the end of December 1991 to R103.9 billion in all currencies (of which R75.2 billion was in rubles) at the end of 1995. The index of real credit declined over this period from 100 percent to 23.6 percent (17.1 percent rubles only). (See figure 2.) Total credit contracted from 31.4 percent of GDP to 11.2 percent during 1991–1995, while ruble credit contracted to 8.1 percent of GDP. Total loanable funds contracted from 68.4 percent of GDP to 16.7 percent of GDP during 1991–1995. The collapse in credit was due to the destruction of household savings through highly negative interest rates during the extremely high inflation years of 1992 and 1993, coupled with massive capital flight and the failure of a real banking system to develop.

The ratio of some broad definition of the money supply to cash in circulation is an indicator of the degree of financial and economic development in a country. The ratio of M_2 to M_0, cash in circulation, declined from about 5:1 in 1991 to 2.7:1 in 1995. (The U.S. ratio of the money supply to currency in circulation is about 12:1.) The decline in real credit went hand in hand with the sharp decline in the ratio of M_2 to cash. To all intents and purposes, Russia increasingly became a cash economy in rubles and dollars (see figure 3).

The collapse of real credit contributed to a contraction of recorded real output to 57 percent of the 1990 level, much deeper than the 30 percent decline during the U.S. depression. The declines in real credit and GDP tracked each other closely during 1991–1995 (see figures 1 and 2).

The contraction of credit dissipated (wiped out is a better phrase) household savings and the country's deposit base. Household deposits, equal to 34 percent of GDP in 1990, fell to 27 percent in 1991, dropped precipitously to 3 percent in 1993, and settled at 4.3 percent at the end of 1995. Banks became irrelevant to the real economy; their credits to enterprises fell from 31 percent of GDP in late 1991 to 8 percent of GDP at the end of 1995. Russian commercial banks (apart from the Savings Bank) were largely irrelevant to the household sector, holding household deposits equivalent to about 1 to 1.5 percent of GDP.

In 1992–1993, real interest rates on deposits were highly negative, −93 percent; in 1994 through early 1995 they were −40 percent. In the aggregate, the banking system literally stole its liabilities—depositors' real funds. (Interest rates turned positive for time deposits during the second half of 1995.)

Household disincentives to maintain ruble deposits were matched by bank disincentives to lend to the real economy. Banks found it more lucrative to engage in foreign exchange transactions, foreign trade servicing, government bonds, interbank lending, and a modest degree of equity and real estate investment.

Russian banks entered 1992 without a debt burden inherited from the past (the debt burden was the government's foreign debt). Unfortunately, the big inflation and highly negative interest rates of 1992 financed a rapid growth in nonperforming debt, up to a third of all loans (see figure 6.) As nonperforming assets constituted an ever-higher share of the banks' balance sheets, they reduced the banks' ability to make new loans. The balance sheets of enterprises became endowed with negative collateral as paper liabilities exceeded paper assets.

Summary

During the immediate post-Soviet years of the Russian Federation, the commercial banking system was a banking system in name only. As mentioned, Russian banks did not accept deposits or make loans their primary activity. Rather, the banks were extensions of the CBR and the government, along with self-oriented profit centers through trading on their own accounts. Let us summarize the situation during 1991–1995:

1. *Banks Served Primarily as Secondary Redistribution Vehicles of Public Funds.* We have previously described the redistributive activities of banks as recipients of cheap CBR credit. After April 1995, new direct CBR credit to commercial banks and the government was banned. To replace it, the Ministry of Finance provided subsidies through the rollover of high-yield bonds. This subsidy was especially generous for large, government-connected banks in which the government held its deposits and through which it conducted its foreign exchange and debt service operations. Banks used government deposits to buy government bonds and kept the difference in interest—a huge sum. Then, selected banks used their growing accumulation of capital to purchase shares of the best energy and other enterprises at subsidized government auctions—the controversial loans-for-shares privatization phase of 1995. Throughout, there was no new source of credit emanating from household deposits.

2. Lack of Deposit Multiplication and Money Creation by Banks. In normal economies, banks create money by multiplying deposits, which increases the ratio of any broad definition of money supply to cash or high-powered base money. In Russia, banks largely shuffled CBR money from one enterprise or government account to another. The activities of banks consisted largely of servicing the current accounts of enterprises, reintermediation in foreign exchange between enterprises for foreign trade operations, foreign exchange arbitrage, government bond operations, interbank lending, and financing capital flight. The effective rollover of enterprise debt and the bailout of nonperforming bank loans by the government prevented the *hidden collective bankruptcy* of both the enterprise and the financial sectors.

3. Lack of Bank Lending to Households. In Russia, banks did not, and still do not, lend to households for home mortgages and consumer purchases. The volume of such credit is minuscule. There is little or no retail banking. (Ordinary Russians do not use checking accounts or credit cards.) On January 1, 1996, total household debt, mainly mortgages, equaled $269 million, equivalent to 0.08 percent of GDP, 0.6 percent of the money stock, 0.2 percent of total bank assets, and about 1 percent of total credit. Credit to enterprises, subsidized by the government and the CBR, consumed 99 percent of total credit. Household lending was absent because all other banking activities were more profitable and a system of mortgages did not exist.

4. The Structure of Loans, Performing and Nonperforming. About 95 percent of all bank loans to the real sector were short term, less than three months in duration. The only source of longer-term loans, which ranged from six months to a year (hardly long term in a normal financial system), was the heavily subsidized, state-owned Savings Bank. Deposits at the Savings

Bank are insured by the government, which permits it to extend a larger part of its loans for more than three months.

During 1992–1995, lending in Russia was somewhat impervious to interest rates. The typical bank-enterprise situation was that banks rolled over short-term loans to enterprises regardless of the interest or inflation rate (especially when enterprises owned their own banks). In a normal economy, interest rates rise or fall with changes in inflation. Insolvent firms find it hard to borrow new funds or renew old loans. Banks are forced to write off bad assets. In Russia, loans were often reissued regardless of firm solvency and independent of either the interest or the inflation rate.

Another factor affecting the structure of loans is nonperforming debt, which would be written off in a normal financial system. By the end of 1995, nonperforming loans were estimated at 28 percent of total ruble credit. The size of bad debt meant that banks had few reserve assets that could be earmarked for long-term lending. Banks required all their spare funds (liquidity) to cover negative cash flow. As a result, banks largely financed working capital and had few funds left over with which to finance investment.

5. Lack of Equity Investment. Russian banks are permitted to function as German-type universal banks. Nonetheless, until 1997, they generally avoided investment in enterprise equity. Capitalization of the Russian stock market during 1995 ranged between $19 and 26 billion, not much more than 5–7 percent of GDP, of which banks held about 30 percent of total equity. Of this 30 percent, about half was held for arbitrage resale to foreigners. The true equity position of banks amounted to about $3 billion, equal to 4 percent of total bank assets and 0.8 percent of GDP.

6. *Insolvency.* Bank insolvency was structural and inherent. Banks were liquid to the extent that continuing government subsidies bailed out banks. The failure to bail out banks would have converted a liquidity crisis into a collective insolvency crash.

Virtually all banks, large and small, were illiquid and technically insolvent, according to a 1995 study by the Moscow-based, Western-funded Institute of Economic Analysis, which analyzed the books of 629 Moscow commercial banks. (Unlike the State Statistical Committee's publication of a broad range of national income accounts data, data on banks are notoriously difficult to obtain.) The study found that small banks were generally undercapitalized. It reported that major banks had about 75 percent of their assets in short-term foreign exchange loans, with up to 85 percent of liabilities in ruble demand deposits earning positive real interest rates, with the nominal exchange rate lagging inflation. This was a bubble waiting to burst, which required the government to bail out (or take equity positions in or both) several leading banks during 1994 and 1995.

Tables 1 and 2 present two different balance sheets for Russia's commercial banks as of January 1, 1996.[2] Indeed, the authors of

2. The data presented in tables 1, 2, 4, and 5 are found in, or derived from, three partially overlapping sources published by the CBR. One is the monthly printed bulletin of banking statistics, which in Russian is *Bulleten Bankovskoi Statistiki.* This bulletin is not collected by U.S. libraries, but it can be purchased directly from the CBR's private information agency. The bulletin contains detailed data on credit extended by commercial banks, along with various categories of assets and liabilities of the banking system. It also provides abridged balance sheets of both the CBR and the commercial banks, as well as a monetary survey based on IMF conventions. This source presents data from January 1993 but contains no comprehensive balance sheets before January 1996.

The second source is the Web site of the CBR. Most of its tables are updated each month. It provides less data on commercial banks than the first source but contains more extensive data on monetary aggregates and CBR reserve positions, along with a detailed balance sheet of the CBR itself. This second source includes data from January 1996. However, the balance sheet of both the CBR

Table 1.   Standard Balance Sheet of Russian Commercial Banks as of January 1, 1996 (all values in billions of current rubles)

Assets		Liabilities	
Reserves	36,712	Demand deposits	69,332
Foreign assets	46,149	Time deposits	69,241
Claims on the government	62,639	Foreign exchange deposits	55,256
Claims on enterprises (performing)	196,247	Government deposits	9,741
Claims on other financial institutions	525	Central Bank credit	8,005
		Bank-issued bills of exchange, equal to quasi–Central Bank credit	11,859
		Foreign liabilities	29,970
		Undistributed liabilities	22,182
Total Assets	342,272	Total Liabilities	275,586
Memorandum item: bank liquidity (nonborrowed reserves)	28,707	Equity	66,688

the *OECD Economic Surveys 1997–1998: Russian Federation*, which contains a special chapter on "Commercial Banking," repeatedly complain of the difficulties in getting accurate information on the balance sheets of the banks. Among other charges,

---

and the commercial banks as of January 1993 exists in other published sources.

The third source is a quarterly statistical journal of the CBR, *Current Trends in the Monetary and Credit Sphere (Tekushchie Tendentsii v Denezhno-Kreditnoi Sfere)*. It contains data for the period before 1993, along with various additional indicators. It can be purchased from the CBR's information agency. This is the only source that published reliable data on net international reserves and a number of other specific items before April 1998.

Taken together, these three sources provide the wherewithal to compile a more accurate set of financial statements for the CBR and the commercial banks than would be possible just using readily available statistical sources found in libraries or in Web sites.

Table 2.   Revised Balance Sheet of Russian Commercial Banks as of January 1, 1996 (all values in billions of current rubles)

Assets		Liabilities	
Reserves and CB deposits	36,712	Demand deposits	69,332
Reserves	23,000	Time deposits	69,241
CB deposits	13,712	Foreign exchange deposits	55,256
Foreign assets	46,149	Government deposits	9,741
Claims on the government	62,639	Central Bank credit	8,005
All claims on enterprises (performing) (equities, loans issued as bank bills of exchange, performing money loans)	174,749	Bank-issued bills of exchange, equal to quasi–Central Bank Credit	16,893
Equities (market value)	30,000	Foreign liabilities	29,970
Loans issued as bank bills of exchange	16,893	Bank bonds (tradeable)	6,093
Money loans (performing)	127,856	Undistributed liabilities	22,182
Nonperforming loans (principal) (for information only)	(15,870)	Loans to bank-owned enterprises (estimated)	40,000
Nonperforming loans (interest) (for information only)	(21,800)	Contingent liabilities: direct government loans to bank-owned enterprises (est.)	5,000
Claims on other financial institutions	525	Contingent liabilities: tax arears (est.)	20,000
		Contingent liabilities: payroll arears (est.)	2,000
Total Assets	320,774	Total Liabilities	353,713
Memorandum item: bank liquidity (nonborrowed reserves)	(1,898)	Equity	(32,939)

the authors state that commercial banks seriously underestimate the share of bad assets in their balances.[3]

Both tables 1 and 2 draw on official Russian sources but present different portraits of the health of the commercial banking system. Table 1 presents what we might call the "standard" balance sheet of the commercial banks. It is published monthly, roughly in this form, by the Central Bank in its official releases and posted on its web site. It contains the standard list of assets and liabilities that appear in the balance sheets of most banks. The left-hand side of the table itemizes the assets of the banks. These include reserves held with the Central Bank, the ruble value of foreign assets (at the exchange rate of the day), claims on the government (holdings of Treasury bills, bonds, and other government financial instruments), claims on enterprises (performing loans), and claims on other financial institutions. As of January 1, 1996, total assets of Russian commercial banks amounted to R343,272 billion. The memorandum item at the bottom indicates that bank liquidity was healthy, amounting to R28,707 billion in nonborrowed reserves.

The right-hand side of the table enumerates the liabilities of the banks. The list is self-explanatory. It includes demand deposits, time deposits, foreign currency deposits, Central Bank credit, bank-issued bills of exchange (see the end of chapter 3 for a discussion of bank-issued bills of exchange and why they amount to quasi–Central Bank credit), foreign liabilities, and undistributed liabilities. Total liabilities sum to R275,586 billion. Subtracting liabilities from assets yields positive equity of R66,688 billion, suggesting that the commercial banking system was in good financial shape at the end of 1995.

3. Organization for Economic Cooperation and Development (OECD), *OECD Economic Surveys 1997–1998: Russian Federation* (Paris: OECD, 1997), p. 91.

We believe that table 1 misrepresents the true situation. With recourse to official figures that required considerably more digging, disaggregation, reaggregation, and estimation, we have attempted to reconstruct a more accurate balance sheet. Table 2 presents this more-comprehensive statement, what we will call the "revised" balance sheet.

In constructing the revised balance sheet, we set out to quantify three basic measures: (1) comprehensive assets, (2) comprehensive liabilities; and (3) the true level of nonborrowed reserves as a measure of liquidity. Let us take each of these in turn.

Comprehensive Assets

When we say that assets should be comprehensive, this means that they consist solely of either performing assets or those that have a positive market value. It means, in effect, pruning out various deadweight (or deadwood) nonperforming assets. The true market value of nonperforming assets is zero. They should be scored as zero and removed, or subtracted, from positive assets. Conversely, some good assets, such as equity in natural resource enterprises, should be significantly revalued over their subsidized sales value (original cost) to the banks on which they appear on the books. Thus, instead of R12,328 billion worth of enterprise equity listed on the books of the banks, we increase that figure to the estimated market value of R30,000 billion on January 1996. Thus some of the numbers in the "revised" balance sheet are lower than on the "standard" balance sheet, while others are higher.

To continue, the official data in the monthly statistical releases of the CBR published as hard-copy bulletins disaggregate bank claims on enterprises by types (enterprise equity, total loans, nonperforming loans [principal], nonperforming loans [interest], loans issued as bank bills of exchange) and allow the precise calculation of enterprise bills of exchange (which are unrecoverable and worthless claims) in the banks' portfolio of assets. It is possible, then, to subtract all nonperforming claims on enterprises from true assets as well as add in the market value premium of performing claims on enterprises in order to arrive at true total assets.

Comprehensive Liabilities

The standard balance sheet of the commercial banks, as presented by the CBR, is incomplete. It uses standard international conventions as employed by the IMF, but it omits several liabilities that are specific to the peculiar Russian banking system. Between the IMF and the CBR, this amounts to a version of "don't ask, don't tell." To arrive at comprehensive liabilities, items must be added or revised.

To begin with, bank-issued bills of exchange should be listed in full, rather than as partial segments that are labeled "monetary instruments." Although they qualify as monetary instruments by the IMF definition, Russian banks also issue what might be classified as "less-qualifying junk monies." Junk monies, regardless of their market quality, are issued by the banks, are credited to enterprises, and represent banks' liability, as well as quasi–central bank credits (because they are issued by banks without using deposits as backing for them). Tradeable bank bonds should also be added to liabilities. The next large item to be added to liabilities is internal loans to bank-owned enterprises. The CBR includes those in assets. Those internal loans can either be subtracted from assets or added to liabilities, which we have done. This (to count them as both assets and liabilities of the banks) generates a more comprehensive accounting.

Other liabilities of bank-owned enterprises should be treated as bank liabilities, especially since there is cross-subsidization and cross-responsibility according to Russian laws. There is no limited liability for Russian banks that separates their liabilities from those of the enterprises they own. In late 1997, when the government desperately needed to collect tax arrears from the largest enterprise debtors, it did not approach enterprises but rather squeezed major banks (e.g., Uneximbank, Russian Credit, etc.) and got paid. In this vein, we also include in comprehensive liabilities what amount to contingent liabilities of the banking system: direct government loans to bank-owned enterprises, tax arrears, and payroll arrears of bank-owned enterprises. In each case, our estimates of these additional liabilities are conservative and minimal.

Nonborrowed Reserves

Nonborrowed reserves should reflect the true volume of domestic currency reserves. First, they should include reserves in coins and currency (central bank notes) only, not book-entry deposits held by banks with the CBR. Book-entry deposits cannot help increase liquidity in terms of cash. To increase liquidity, the CBR would have to print (or mint) additional money. Commercial bank deposits with the central bank may be called reserves in some accounting sense, as banks can resort to them to force the central bank to print new money. This is, in fact, the reason that banks place book-entry deposits with the central bank: to exchange on demand an illiquid, book-entry value (which represents merely a pledge not to lend this amount to enterprises at this moment) for liquid, hard cash printed by the central bank. This arrangement keeps structurally illiquid Russian banks liquid at any moment in time.

This arrangement potentially undermines the monetary base, however, because banks can, on demand, force the CBR to print as much money as they deposit (and they can, if need be, deposit the entire stock of broad money, less currency in circulation). But those bank deposits with the CBR are not reserves in the standard monetary sense of bank reserves and thus should be subtracted from the central bank notion of reserves reported on the balance sheet (again, the IMF did not ask, and the central bank did not tell). Second, bank-issued bills of exchange granted to enterprises as credit are banknotes loaned without deposits to back them. Issuing such credits by banks is equivalent to receiving central bank credits, in notes and coins, and relending them to enterprises. This is how banks behaved, except that they did not receive central bank credit as they issued bills of exchange. When U.S. financial institutions issue private monies (e.g., travelers' checks), they exchange these notes for official central bank notes, which means that the ultimate notes are created by the central bank, not by the issuer of private monies.

In Russia, banks became the autonomous and ultimate issuers of notes, on par with the central bank and its equivalents. They self-accommodate and self-issue central bank credit to themselves this way. Those bank notes must be subtracted from banks' reserves, along with direct central bank credit to banks on the books, to arrive at the true volume of nonborrowed reserves. This is because under normal conditions banks would have to purchase central bank notes in the amount equal to their privately issued notes. Since they cannot acquire them from households and enterprises (neither households nor enterprises buy bank notes, which are bad monies, with good money, which is central bank notes), the issue of such notes by banks is equivalent to the quasi purchase of central bank notes from the central bank, or a forced central bank credit. By subtracting items such as bank deposits with the central bank from bank reserves listed on the central bank's standard balance sheets, central bank credit to banks, and bank-issued bills of exchange, we arrive at the true amount of nonborrowed reserves of the Russian banking system, which happens to be perpetually negative.

With these comments in hand, let us derive the revised balance sheet of the commercial banks, beginning with the assets. A portion of what is listed as reserves held with the CBR is, in fact, deposits. The true level of reserves requires subtracting these deposits from official reserves. We have performed this exercise in the second and third rows of table 2, which yields reserves of R23,000 billion, compared with the simple figure of R35,712 billion. This disaggregates but does not reduce total assets. Foreign assets are the same in both tables. To obtain the true value of performing assets, some R174,749 billion, we add together R30,000 billion in our augmented market value of equities held by the banks, R16,893 billion in loans issued as bank bills of exchange, and R127,856 billion in genuine performing loans. (The value of genuine performing loans was obtained by subtracting all nonmoney claims on enterprises, at market value, from total claims on enterprises and then subtracting nonperforming loans, both principal and interest.) For information purposes, in the revised balance sheet we show the value of nonperforming loans for both principal and interest. Total assets amount to R320,774 billion, which is considerably lower than the corresponding figure in table 1.

Even more adjustments must be made on the liability side of the balance sheet. The first four entries in table 2 are identical with those in table 1. The actual level of bank-issued bills of exchange is higher than the figure that appears in the simple balance sheet of table 1. The difference is that the standard CBR balance sheet uses a narrow IMF definition of monetary instruments whereas the monthly bulletin lists all bank-issued bills of exchange, including less liquid ones.

We also include several categories of liabilities that are missing from table 1. These include tradeable bank bonds, loans issued to enterprises owned by banks, and three contingent liabilities: direct government loans to bank-owned enterprises, tax arrears, and payroll arrears. These revisions increase total liabilities to R353,713 billion, well above the corresponding figure in table 1. The result is that banks have a negative equity of R32,939 billion. Thus table 2 presents a completely different picture from that in table 1: The system is insolvent, rather than in good health. We also add, as described above, the revised value of nonborrowed reserves: minus R1,898 billion, highly negative.

7. *The Relationship between the Banking System and the Real Sector.* The banking system—a winding maze of borrower ownership of banks, insider lending, rollover of bad loans, misallocation of credit, lack of competitive credit markets, and lack of long-term investment and credit—impeded the development of the new private sector and the restructuring of potentially viable enterprises. Misallocation of credit and depletion of real deposits deprived productive users of credit and investment. A vicious circle developed that perpetuated bad credit, reinforced financial repression, and depressed the real sector. Most emerging private firms were forced to self-finance or organize informal arrangements with individuals.

8. *The Relationship between the Banking System, the Budget, and Tax Policy.* In normal countries, the budget of the government and the budgets of households and firms are separate. In Russia, the two have been blurred. The government—the Ministry of Finance, the Executive Office of the President, the CBR, the eighty-nine regional governments of the Russian Federation—all use their resources to subsidize "private" economic activity.

To raise the additional revenue required given insufficient tax collections, the CBR granted credits to the government. Almost all of the 1994 budget deficit (a staggering 10.4 percent of GDP) was financed directly by the CBR. The explosion in credit fueled inflation and eroded the exchange-rate value of the currency, resulting in a revised central bank law that appeared to limit direct CBR financing of the budget to R5 trillion.

In response to reduced CBR credits, the government financed its deficit through a second means: the issue of government bonds. The government began to sell three-month Treasury bills (GKOs in Russian) in earnest in June 1994. The volume of GKO sales rose sharply in the spring of 1995 (the government financed 70 percent of its 1995 deficit through short-term bonds). Outstanding government debt more than doubled over this brief period, to constitute 8 percent of GDP. A growing stock of short-term debt drove up interest rates on new and refinanced issues to 60 percent and higher.

High interest rates created a perverse incentive. To the extent that firms and individuals met their tax obligations, the government's need to borrow would correspondingly decline. Noncompliance, however, became enormously profitable. Firms that withheld tax payments, when in fact they had the funds to remit, could earn 60 percent interest on government bonds. This was an enormous incentive to delay tax payments, buy bonds, collect 60 percent interest, and then pay back taxes with interest earnings. The government—happy to get money however and whenever it was remitted—was grateful that someone was buying domestic debt. The explosion in GKOs carried over into 1996, which was a year of exceptionally high yields on government debt. Indeed, the commercial banking system as a whole derived about 70 percent of its income from government securities in 1996.

CHAPTER THREE

The Emergence of a Resource-Based Monetary System, Hamstrung by the Persistence of Ersatz Banks: 1996–1997

The Russian government's budget was the defining hallmark of International Monetary Fund (IMF) concern. The Ministry of Finance, the CBR, and the Russian government became bound by terms set by the IMF, the Paris Club of creditor nations, and the foreign aid programs of Germany, France, and the United States. The receipt of each month's tranche of a three-year IMF loan of $10 billion, along with direct foreign loans, required meeting performance criteria on budget deficits, inflation, the level of net international reserves, ceilings on net domestic assets, and limits on central bank lending to the federal and regional governments. From time to time, the IMF withheld its monthly transfer when Russia failed to meet its stipulated targets.

Whether the CBR would have developed some semblance of a real monetary system without prodding from the IMF is not clear. The CBR had previously tried and failed to get control of the money supply, the ruble, and inflation. In any event, Russia's dire need for international financial assistance put an end to the indiscriminate issue of central bank credit and currency.

EXPERIMENTING WITH THE
CREATION OF A MONETARY SYSTEM

The IMF established performance criteria with the Russian government that stipulated targets for net international reserves (NIR) and net domestic assets (NDA), which together define the monetary base. Restricting the growth of the monetary base helped bring inflation, as measured by the consumer price index, down to 11 percent (almost single-digit levels using the GDP price deflator measure) by the end of 1997. The CBR began to close small insolvent commercial banks and temporarily took over larger banks as needed. In short, Russia got on track to test a real monetary system through which it could conduct normal monetary policy operations.

Serendipity: Prelude to a Monetary System

Beginning in mid-1994, the Russian government, together with the CBR, considered using the exchange rate as a nominal anchor to achieve financial stabilization, a policy that seemed to have worked with considerable success in the Czech Republic, Slovakia, and Poland in the 1990s and Israel in the mid-1980s, to give but four examples. For Russia, this would amount to fixing the nominal exchange rate of the ruble to a strong foreign currency, such as the dollar, to discipline the CBR's conduct of monetary policy. Fixing the exchange rate, or creating a narrow band around which the ruble would be permitted to fluctuate, would, it was thought, help dampen inflationary expectations among holders of rubles, thereby reducing the velocity of money and inflation, even as prior monetary expansion temporarily continued to inflate the price level. As inflation continued in the face of a fixed nominal exchange rate, the real exchange rate would begin to appreciate, which would further increase ruble demand

and further reduce inflation. If, at the same time, the CBR significantly slowed the increase in the money supply, inflation could be brought down quickly and a stable monetary regime could emerge.

However, to achieve and maintain a stable monetary regime, defined as the attainment of relatively stable prices, budget deficits cannot be financed by printing money. Any budget deficit, preferably as low as possible, would have to be financed exclusively by debt. There could be no central bank refinancing of commercial banks except the emergency provision of liquidity, no open market operations with government bonds as an instrument of monetary expansion, and certainly no monetization of quasi-fiscal deficits such as interenterprise arrears or rollover of enterprise defaults on bank loans.

To be effective, the new monetary regime would also require a sound, independent banking system capable of raising funds from the household sector to supply credit to the productive sector. This regime would also require a low current-account deficit or a current-account surplus to sustain the exchange-rate peg and some initial foreign exchange reserves to start the system.

Thus the Russian government entertained the idea of the fixed exchange-rate corridor in conjunction with moving from central bank credit to debt financing the budget deficit. But the government knew that its banks were insolvent and could not mobilize household deposits and that the Russian people held their deposits in foreign currency in their mattresses. Moreover, the fledgling market for government debt could not handle even a slowly growing amount of government bonds. Thus in September 1994 the government confronted a severe liquidity crisis. It was forced to rely on *foreign* debt financing of its still large budget deficit and various other debts in the economy (including the ever-growing enterprise arrears). Effectively, the Russian government said to Western governments and the IMF that, if they did not like

Russian inflation, they would have to supply dollars to reduce the need to print rubles to patch Russia's fiscal and quasi-fiscal holes and, at the same time, provide foreign exchange reserves to support the new exchange-rate regime.

The Russian government presented this blueprint to the IMF October 3–5, 1994, with a request for $16 billion. However audacious, this proposition was not without foundation: Many times since 1992 Western governments and the IMF pledged to Russia various astronomical sums of foreign aid and, specifically, a multibillion-dollar stabilization fund. So the Russians called the Western bluff and ambushed the IMF in Madrid.

The plan lacked both fiscal and monetary credibility. The budget deficit was forecast at 8 percent of GDP (and was actually 11 percent of GDP), excluding quasi-fiscal deficits. As a result, the IMF put the request on hold pending further negotiations. On October 11, 1994, there was a run on the dollar in Moscow, and the ruble lost 27 percent of its nominal value, although it soon recovered. The collapse in the ruble was a shock with political repercussions and a policy watershed.

The central bank raised interest rates to 170 percent in October 1994, 180 percent in November 1994, and 200 percent in January 1995. These high rates reduced credit to enterprises and increased placement of government bonds at annualized yields hovering between 80 and 100 percent. The most important measure, however, was the resumption of forced loans, abolished after the death of Joseph Stalin in 1953. The government issued special short-term bonds, or promissory notes (called KOs), which was a forced subscription on enterprises and banks, and imputed them in lieu of outlays to budget recipients. That drastic reduction of money outlays and the growth of fiscal arrears cut the budget deficit to 4 percent in early 1995. The parliament adopted the budget in March 1995 with an estimated 5.5 percent deficit, which was to be fully financed by bond issues without central bank credit. The growth of money supply decelerated (but still remained at about 8 percent a month).

At the same time, the CBR commenced a series of rapid devaluations, while Russia's current-account surplus expanded. Foreign exchange reserves doubled, from $4 billion to $8 billion during the first half of 1995. In the spring of 1995, the exchange rate stabilized and even began to appreciate. Meanwhile, the IMF reconsidered its previous rejection and signed a $6.7 billion one-year package. In July 1995, the government and the central bank fixed the exchange rate in a narrow band. A new monetary system thus came into being one year after the idea first circulated inside government circles.

This heroic effort would not have been durable or sustainable beyond a year, a year and a half at best, save for an unforeseen and completely unrelated parallel development on the banking and privatization fronts. In another corner of Moscow, oblivious to and unknown to the IMF and the Russian government, a small group of Western investment bankers of Russian descent, spun off from the Russian office of CS First Boston, and their Russian partners, from an obscure but rapidly growing Uneximbank (the private United Export Import Bank),[1] developed a brilliant scheme to fill the government's desperate need to finance the deficit.

Here is how the scheme was designed to work. The government would consolidate its considerable but dispersed demand deposits in a small number of trusted, loyal banks. These banks would issue low-interest loans from these funds (the government's own deposits) to the government in exchange for an option to purchase stock in valuable, state-owned, natural resource enterprises. Since these options to buy are not initially the actual sales

---

1. Uneximbank was created from the frozen and transferred assets of the collapsed, state-owned Soviet Bank for Foreign Trade.

of real assets but only stock options held in trust by the banks in the event the government failed to repay the loans, this transfer could be conducted at very low equity prices. These low prices would make the existing government demand deposits sufficient for conducting the financial transfer operations on the books. The government could list these low-interest paper loans as additional budget revenues (adding the loans to its deposits, even though it was a single source of funds), thereby appearing to reduce its budget deficit and thus qualifying for the receipt of real loans from the IMF. The actual amount of domestically raised government funds would not change, but its paper deposits would multiply by those financial shenanigans—self-borrowing and self-lending through the banks. It is hard to blame the banks for taking real resources off the government's hands at bargain basement prices as they helped the government get real foreign currency from the IMF!

Meanwhile, the trusted, loyal banks obtained new financial resources as the option to purchase shares in oil, metals, and other natural resource enterprises endowed them with real assets and a steady flow of income from either dividends or resale of these assets. As long as the government retained the option to return the loans to the banks and recall the enterprise shares, this meant giving the banks a direct money subsidy instead of a subsidy in the form of real assets, which was not feasible given IMF constraints on credit creation and the continued budget deficit.

This scheme, euphemistically called *options auctions* or *collateral auctions* in Russia and *loans for shares* in the Western press, went into effect in late August 1995, just after the exchange-rate band was set and right in the middle of the ensuing banking-liquidity crisis. The truth was that the banking system was insolvent and that the government was running a larger-than-reported budget deficit and an even larger quasi-fiscal deficit. The government could not possibly have financed these deficits and sustained the banking system without continuous monetization and inflationary finance. Debt financing was not really feasible except through central bank repurchase of government bonds. The banks also did not have funds to purchase enterprise shares on the real market at the market price, which is why the option sales, or loans for shares, hiddenly financed by the government itself, raised five times more revenue in 1995 and early 1996, despite their low prices, than all other actual privatization.

But the significance of this development, which went beyond the fiscal bookkeeping and bank recapitalization, revealed itself when the equity and bond markets broadly opened to foreigners in 1996–1997 and the resale of shares and bonds became the principal source of money creation instead of the repurchase of bonds by the CBR. The rise in share values helped sustain the new monetary regime after 1996.

The above transfer-lending process operated until September 1996. Thereafter the government, predictably, did not repay the "loans" and allowed the banks, which held the shares in "trust," to purchase them at prices only nominally above the loans. At the same time, the government also started to sell to the banks, through closed auctions, large portfolios of shares in the remaining natural resource state-owned enterprises, instead of offering shares to the public directly on the stock market. By that time, the ruble was convertible into foreign currency on the capital account, albeit with some restrictions. The government bond market was partially open to foreigners, who were permitted to purchase up to 30 percent of ruble-denominated debt. The Russian equity markets were fully open to all potential purchasers.

The banks began to resell their assets in equity on the stock market to foreign investors and used the proceeds to purchase government bonds. The government also sold debt to foreigners and entered the dollar-denominated foreign bond market, issuing eurobonds. Those efforts enabled the government to finance its debt, recapitalize the banks and allowed the banks to purchase high-yield government debt that sustained their own operational liquidity—using foreign capital inflows as the source of new funds. Access to foreign funds throughout 1997 sustained an otherwise unsustainable monetary regime.

Even though the banking system remained afloat through real resource recapitalization and resale to foreigners, the monetary regime became unsustainable because high bond yields during 1995–1996 required rolling over a steadily growing debt (see below for details). Both the total debt and the costs of debt service continuously increased. These higher costs could be sustained only through the repurchase of bonds by the CBR and monetizing the debt. The semifixed (crawling peg) exchange-rate anchor of the emerging monetary system could not have withstood this monetization without large capital inflows. The ruble would have undergone a sharp devaluation, high inflation would have set in, and any kind of stable monetary framework would have gone up in printed paper.

What saved the day for the monetary system were the foreign investors who bought stocks at market prices, giving the banks and other enterprises substantial capital gains, which became the means of recapitalizing the banks from late 1996 into 1997. The government was relieved of the need to provide high-yield bonds to the banks as the vehicle for recapitalization because it was able to secure foreign sources of funding for more than a third of its debt. Short-term interest rates fell, CBR repurchases of bonds declined, and the growth in the money supply became compatible with the growth in real foreign resources (whether a return of Russian capital flight or genuine foreign capital).

Focus on Ruble Stability

The central plank of Russian monetary policy during 1996–1997 was the relative stability of the ruble in the quest to reduce inflation, a process difficult to achieve overnight. During the transition phase to lower inflation, the CBR pursued a low nominal depreciation of the ruble against the dollar to offset higher domestic Russian inflation. When necessary, the CBR entered the currency markets, buying foreign currency to avoid ruble appreciation as in 1997, which witnessed an increase in the inflow of foreign capital and some repatriation of flight capital. As a result, net international reserves rose from $0.6 billion in January 1997 to $11 billion in July but fell to about $9 billion in November and to $4.2 billion in January 1998.[2]

The CBR's purchasing of dollars with rubles in 1997 was a marked change from previous years, when the issue of rubles resulted in rapid currency depreciation, inflation, and a fall in reserves. This time, the issue of rubles was driven by the demand for Russian currency and ruble-denominated assets. The Russian stock market was the world's best-performing equity market in percentage gains in both 1996 and 1997. The government officially de-dollarized the economy, requiring that all legal payments be made in rubles. The growing strength of the ruble led the government to announce in mid-1997 its intention, beginning January 1, 1998, to lop three zeros off the ruble, redenominating the currency at a rate of one new ruble to one thousand old rubles. To avoid the panic that took place during previous currency measures, the government announced that both old and new

---

2. Net international reserves are defined as gross international reserves minus short-term international liabilities of the monetary authorities (all liabilities shorter than one year of the CBR and the Ministry of Finance). By definition, short-term foreign liabilities include the outstanding value of IMF loans, even though their duration may exceed one year. The difference between gross and net international reserves consists largely of IMF lending. Thus real net international reserves are actually higher than listed net international reserves because a portion of Russia's short-term foreign liabilities is not really short term. Net reserves peaked at about $9 billion in the fall of 1997, which was a historic high and which reflected the removal of forward cover offered by the CBR through the former S-Account structures through which foreign investors bought and sold dollar-based Russian securities.

rubles would circulate as legal tender during all of 1998 and that old rubles could be exchanged for new rubles through 2002.

The "Asian contagion" that afflicted Thailand, Indonesia, Malaysia, the Philippines, and Korea beginning in midsummer 1997 spread to Russia's currency and financial markets in early December 1997. The CBR spent more than $5 billion in foreign reserves of its $23 billion gross cache in an attempt to defend the ruble, while trying to keep its refinance rate at what was then a relatively low 18 percent (down from 48 percent in January to 42 percent in February, 36 percent in April, and 24 percent in June). As reserves dwindled, and with some persuasive advice from one of the inventors of the loans-for-shares scheme, Boris Jordan, chief executive officer of Renaissance Capital, the CBR realized that it was more important to defend the hard-won gains in ruble stability than to maintain low interest rates and protect low debt service costs. The CBR recognized that the risk to the banking system, heavily burdened with dollar liabilities, was too great to permit those liabilities to rise sharply in ruble terms. At one point, the entire commercial banking system teetered on the brink of financial implosion. Equally important, the government debt market was at risk of a massive sell-off of bonds, as investors stood ready to dump bonds to hedge against ruble devaluation if yields did not increase to compensate for the risk of devaluation. The CBR withdrew from the money market and let interest rates rise above 30 percent, which kept the ruble within its predetermined annual exchange-rate band against the dollar. It also adjusted the band to plus or minus 15 percent on either side of the rate.

The creation of a commercial banking system has been the most tortuous and least successful part of the Russian reform process. The government and the CBR have attempted to sustain the banking system by numerous methods of endowing banks with capital, with the ultimate goal of financing real enterprises with credit. In the face of IMF restrictions on the CBR's issuing credit, the CBR was finding it increasingly difficult to inject new capital resources into the banks, which would be a monstrous problem were the entire system to crash under the weight of its dollar liabilities. The decision to let banks maintain some degree of solvency in their balance sheets, in the form of higher interest rates on government debt, simultaneously protecting the ruble, won out over devaluation. The price would be another post-ponement of the long-awaited beginning of growth, as higher interest rates would reduce real investment and drain additional resources into refinancing government debt.

The Growth of Domestic Debt

Limits on CBR credits during the past few years have forced the government to rely on debt financing in the form of short-term Treasury bills (GKOs) and longer-term federal loan bonds (OFZs). By mid-1997, the outstanding stock of GKOs and OFZs reached R311.4 trillion ($52 billion), or 12.1 percent of annual-ized June GDP, rising to R385 trillion ($64 billion) by January 1998. The stock of GKOs and OFZs has risen steadily, from 2 percent of GDP in January 1995 to about 4.4 percent of GDP in January 1996, 10.5 percent of GDP in January 1997, and 13.9 percent by 1998.

Although this is a small percentage (internal debt as a per-centage of GDP) compared with advanced Western economies, the stark difference is that almost all of it must be refunded every half year. The prospect of refunding at decreasing interest rates in 1998 was waylaid by the sharp backup in interest rates in December 1997, meaning that a huge percentage of the govern-ment budget is consumed by interest payments. If higher interest rates remain in force in 1998, it will require an additional 2 percent or more of GDP, beyond that previously estimated, to fund the government's deficit. (There is no long-term government debt market in Russia.)

As a result of the shift from CBR credits to the issue of government debt, debt financing has created a vibrant, and profitable, market in Russian debt. The average maturity of GKOs and OFZs rose from 108.2 days at the end of 1995 to 207.2 days in mid-1997. As maturities lengthened, interest rates declined, from an annualized rate of 200 percent in mid-1996 to 18 percent in late 1997. When the "Asian financial contagion" hit Russian markets in December 1997, the CBR let interest rates rise back above 30 percent (above 40 percent in early 1998) until the reduction to the mid-30s in March 1998.

Foreign Participation in the Domestic Debt Market

To help finance the budget deficit, in early 1996 the government permitted foreigners to purchase a specified share of the total value of bonds at primary auctions. However, it restricted the maximum interest rate for nonresidents to 20–25 percent in dollar terms compared with 70 percent and higher in ruble terms for residents, though this gap steadily narrowed. Special S-Accounts were established, which required that foreigners buy future contracts for delivery of dollars with a one-month wait if they wished to sell government bills and bonds and repatriate the proceeds in foreign currency. The CBR abolished S-Account restrictions on January 1, 1998, permitting instant repatriation. Between August 15 and October 15, 1996, international investment in the GKO Treasury bill market was about $2.1 billion. International investors added greatly to their stock of GKO and OFZ issues from the end of 1996 through 1997, for the compound rate of return was extremely high by global standards. At the end of 1997, foreigners held $14.5 billion in GKOs and $1.8 billion in OFZs.

As the Asian currency crisis unfolded, foreigners cashed in, re-patriating about $1.3 billion of GKOs between October 1997 and January 1998.

As inflation fell, thanks to the growing success of the CBR in getting control over the money supply, several Russian banks and large firms, such as largely government-owned Gazprom and Lukoil, began to borrow abroad in 1996 and early 1997. In some respects, this was tantamount to foreign borrowing by differently named branches of the government and the CBR, as the CBR remained the lender of last resort for all Russian foreign debt. This process of foreign borrowing stalled temporarily in late 1997 when the currency and stock markets of Asia collapsed.

Private Holdings of Foreign Currency

Russia's official net international reserves are dwarfed by private holdings of foreign currency. Russians do not trust their government, especially when it comes to currency. The collapse of the ruble during 1991–1995 and the loss of deposits shattered public confidence in the ruble and in the banks. In January 1998, net domestic assets of the CBR stood at R141.2 trillion, net international reserves at $4.2 billion, and the monetary base at R164.5 trillion (about $27.4 billion at the exchange rate of the day). Russian households were estimated to hold in the neighborhood of $40 billion or more in U.S. banknotes, or nearly ten times the level of net reserves and well over 100 percent of the dollar value of both ruble notes and net domestic assets.

There is no shortage of hard currency in Russia, but there is a problem in converting the bulk of it into investment, either directly into dollars or via conversion into rubles. The Russian government officially de-dollarized the economy in the hope that the exclusive use of rubles for retail transactions would reduce velocity and inflation. But dollars remain important in Russia, as evidenced by the massive capital flight and accumulated stocks under mattresses. Russia has consistently run a large trade surplus—$17 billion in 1994, $20.4 billion in 1995, $26.9 billion in 1996, and $19.8 billion in 1997—although rising imports have reduced the current account surplus, which includes trade in both goods and services, to single-digit levels in 1997 (and the current-account surplus turned negative during the second half of 1997).[3] Beginning January 1, 1998, the government imposed a new 2 percent tax on money converted from dollars to rubles and from rubles to dollars to discourage Russians from acquiring additional dollars in the first place.

An enormous stock of potential foreign assets is in private hands that are not part of the official accounts of the country. There is, unfortunately, little likelihood that the government will persuade holders of those dollars to put them to work in the country's ersatz banks, which is another compelling reason to establish real banks.

Foreign Investment

To date, direct foreign investment (DFI) has played a limited role in the Russian economy. Most foreign capital inflows have taken the form of purchases of GKOs, OFZs, and equities. During 1991–1995, cumulative DFI in Russia amounted to about $5 billion, compared with, say, $7 billion in much smaller Hungary. The first promise of large-scale DFI occurred when Uneximbank joined with American financier George Soros and Deutsche Morgan Grenfell to win the auction for Svyazinvest in July 1997. This was followed by two additional alliances: (1) BP with Sidanco/

---

3. Individual purchases of foreign goods by pseudotourists, who are in fact "shuttle traders," enter the service accounts even though those are imports of real goods. The value of that trade is in the billions of dollars.

Uneximbank and (2) Royal Dutch Shell with Gazprom and Lukoil, each formed to bid for Rosneft, the last remaining large state-owned oil company.

Between 1991 and 1997, total DFI amounted to $9.7 billion. Total DFI and portfolio investment, as of January 1998, stood at $36.2 billion. Direct foreign investment thus contributed about 27 percent of foreign investment in equities and enterprises.

Enterprise Arrears

The evidence presented in chapter 2 demonstrated that the growth in enterprise arrears (EAs) was the chief determinant of monetary policy during 1991–1995. The situation changed markedly during 1996–1997, the second phase of Russia's monetary development.

Russia is beset with numerous arrears: enterprise arrears, tax arrears, and wage arrears in the public and nonpublic sectors. President Yeltsin issued an order in 1997 to eliminate public sector wage arrears by year's end and largely accomplished that goal, thanks to foreign loans and overdue tax payments from several large Russian enterprises. His edict did not apply to the much larger stock of wage arrears owed to nongovernment employees. But in 1998 payroll arrears were a contributing issue to Yeltsin's sacking his cabinet.

In chapter 2 we demonstrated that enterprises used interenterprise, wage, and tax arrears as a means of securing government subsidies. Table 3 shows that a change in the monetary regime had no impact on the expansion of all these arrears. The table itemizes arrears on January 1, 1994, in the midst of the old accommodative monetary regime in which a ruble of interenterprise credit resulted in a corresponding ruble increase in money issue. The table compares the level of arrears, both in absolute

Table 3. Arrears in Nominal (Billion Rubles) and Real Terms
(January 1994 = 100)

	1/1/94	1/1/96	Real	1/1/98	Real
Stock of receivables in arrears	R35,957	R289,300	110.4	R676,400	190.9
Tax arrears (including payroll taxes)	3,028	86,800	393.3	316,601*	1,061.1
Payroll arrears	815	13,380	225.3	52,637†	655.4
Stock of promissory notes (est.)	10,000	75,000	102.9	250,000	253.7
Memorandum item: Bank credit‡	30,019	185,975	85.0	255,607	86.4

*R554,900 billion, with fines and penalties
†R54,499 billion on February 1, 1998, and R57,768 billion on March 1, 1998
‡Not fully comparable because 1994 does not include loans in foreign currencies. A full comparison would show more decline in real terms in 1995–97. Bank credit is included in the table for illustrative purposes only. It does not constitute arrears.
Sources: Central Bank of Russia and State Statistical Committee, various releases.

and real terms for January 1, 1996, and late 1997 under the new monetary regime, using 1994 as the base year.

During 1996–1997, unpaid receivables nearly doubled, tax arrears (without fines and penalties) nearly tripled, and payroll arrears almost tripled in real terms. Promissory notes, or *veksels* (see below), increased two and a half times in value. The figures for bank credit are not strictly comparable in that 1994 does not include loans in foreign currencies. The real comparisons thus overstate the level of bank credit; the decline would be much sharper if only ruble loans were included for 1996 and 1997 or if dollars were included in the data for 1994.

The continued rise in enterprise arrears, but with the relative decline in bank financing as a percentage of enterprise liabilities, reflects, first, the phasing out of CBR credits to enterprises (which accounted for 7 percent of total enterprise liabilities in 1994) and, second, the emergence of tight monetary conditions, which resulted in a rise in real interest rates. In response to tight credit conditions, enterprises manufactured their own financing through tax arrears, payroll arrears, and so forth. The difference in the past two years, compared with 1991–1995, is that arrears have not driven monetary policy; rather, they have affected the country's public finances, forcing up the government's costs of servicing public debt. In the long run, sustained economic growth depends on reducing and ultimately eliminating the arrears problem.

THE PERSISTENCE OF ERSATZ BANKS

At the risk of undue repetition, it must be repeated that real banks accept deposits and make loans, a point taught in every elementary economics course. Russian commercial banks hold few deposits. The state Savings Bank, which holds large deposits, makes few loans. By definition, neither the commercial banks nor the Savings Bank are banks or financial intermediaries. Rather, Russian banks are akin to business enterprises but shuffle financial instruments for their own profit instead of producing real goods and services.

An attempt at running a real monetary system in 1995 forced a change in the business activities of Russian banks. They switched from interbank and private-sector credits (though largely to their own captive, often money-losing enterprises or to the enterprises of which they were captive) from CBR resources toward operations in government securities. As interest rates of government bills rose (amounting to annualized rates of 163.7 percent in 1994 and 159.3 percent in 1995), the share of GKOs in the total assets of the banking system rose from 8.5 percent at the end of 1994 to 31 percent at the end of 1997 (see figure 7).

It is interesting to compare 1993–1994 with the three years encompassing 1995–1997. During the first two years, the budget deficit (excluding short-term debt service payments) was respectively 10.4 and 10.7 percent of GDP, while the total deficit came to 10.4 and 11.4 percent (the latter figure includes short-term debt service equal to 0.7 percent of GDP). During 1995–1997, the annual deficit ranged between 3.0 and 3.6 percent of GDP (although adding in debt service payments increased the total deficit to 4.8–7.6 percent for the three years). Interest payments as a percentage of GDP on short-term government debt rose from 0.7 percent in 1994 to 1.8 percent in 1995 to 3 percent in 1996 and to 4 percent in 1997. Since banks derived the bulk of their earnings from interest on government bonds, the banks were

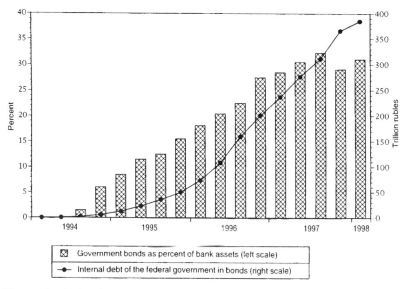

Figure 7. Federal Government Debt and the Share of Government Securities in Bank Assets, Russia, 1994–1998 (quarterly data).
Sources: Central Bank of Russia and Russian State Committee on Statistics, various releases.

effectively recapitalized to the tune of several percentage points of GDP between 1995 and 1997, which still did not make them solvent.

Yields on GKOs, along with yields on subsequently issued OFZs, began to decline in mid-1996. This decline created severe problems throughout the banking system. Many banks (370) were liquidated by the CBR, and many other small banks were merged with one another or into larger institutions. At the end of June 1997, 742 banks had their operating licenses withdrawn by the CBR and were awaiting liquidation. (These small banks, although many in number, represented only 2 percent of the assets of the banking system.)

As GKO yields declined, the stock market came to the rescue. Between mid-1996, after President Yeltsin's reelection, and the end of 1997, the Russian stock market was the best-performing market in the world in percentage terms. Russian banks stocked up on equities, which helped improve their profits and balance sheets. The stock market tailed off sharply in the fourth quarter of 1997 but was still up substantially at year's end.

Another source of profit for the banks was operating the government payments system and Russian customs accounts. At the end of 1997, the government removed both flows from the commercial banks and placed them directly with the Treasury but in 1998 returned the customs accounts to the commercial banks.

As always, the hope is that banks will begin to intermediate household savings to the corporate sector, instead of channeling household funds to the government and government subsidies to enterprises, thus starting the growth process.[4] That is, of course,

---

4. "Banks [are] producers of money. . . . The existence of banks enables productive enterprises to acquire money balances without raising capital from ultimate wealth-owners [the households]. Instead of selling claims (bonds or equities) to them, it [the enterprise] can sell its claims to banks, getting money in exchange: in the phrase that was once so common in textbooks on money,

the big question and the subject of chapter 4. But first it is necessary to set the banks in the context of the real economy. This brings us to the dominant Russian economic institution known as FIGs, the acronym for financial-industrial groups.

Financial-Industrial Groups

There is a big difference between nominally privatizing enterprises and forcing them to behave as real private enterprises in a marketlike setting.[5] The Russian voucher process of privatization gave control over enterprises to managers and, to a much lesser extent, to workers and outside funds. Those who gained control were primarily interested in seizing assets for short-term gains, given the insecurity of property in Russia, rather than reforming the enterprises into profitable, value-adding businesses.

Establishing FIGs was the brainchild of the government, reflecting the execution of state policy toward specific sectors or enterprises. The idea was that banks would act as middlemen between the government and firms, funneling subsidies and state loans from the government to enterprises. This arrangement also held out the promise of converting the financing of business itself into a commercial enterprise. In the first generation of FIGs, the enterprises owned the banks, not the other way around.

The government hoped to use FIGs to rationalize energy and resources production and other major industries and sectors. But the model failed on two counts. Russia did not have sufficient

---

the bank coins specific liabilities into generally accepted liabilities." Milton Friedman, "The Quantity Theory of Money—a Restatement," in Milton Friedman, ed., *Studies in the Quantity Theory of Money* (Chicago: University of Chicago Press, 1956), p. 14.

5. This segment draws on a cover story, "Out of the Ashes," that appeared in the November 1996 issue of *Business Central Europe*, pp. 9–11.

funds to finance the modernization of industry, and the FIGs were unable to manage their companies efficiently.

FIGs were turned upside down in 1995. The process of transformation was the loans-for-shares scheme implemented by the leading banks. On the transformed FIG model, the underlying assumption (perhaps hope is the better word) was that selling controlling stakes in companies to competent commercial banks would put the firms in the hands of the few people qualified to restructure them financially, who would hire Western managers to run them efficiently.

By late 1996, three major FIGs emerged: Interros, closely linked to Uneximbank; the Alfa Group, a private partnership developed by a group of domestic entrepreneurs linked to Alfa Bank; and Menatep, linked to Menatep Bank. Uneximbank acquired Norilsk Nickel and Sidanco, while Menatep got Yukos, a large oil company. (Examples of purely industrial FIGs include Lukoil and Gazprom, the large oil and gas companies.)

The new FIG model requires that the banks get controlling stakes in the firms in their groups, drag them forcibly into the market economy, and gain access to Western capital. For example, in 1997, Uneximbank attracted more than $500 million in capital from BP in the sale of 10 percent of its oil-related firm, Sidanco. The banks, if successful, will fix up and ultimately sell off to real private investors viable firms that add, not subtract, value to the real economy. The banks, in this model, are the equivalent of investment banks, not industrial conglomerates. As the process of fixing and selling off enterprises picks up steam, real growth would follow.

The risk, of course, is that a handful of dominant FIGs will simply build up monopoly positions and fend off real competition or that a few banks will want to control as many industrial assets as possible but not make the necessary investments in capital and management to restructure and make profitable their subsidiary value-subtracting or stagnant enterprises. Another risk is that, in the rush to gain control of as many assets as possible, the banks will overextend themselves and that one or more large banks might fail. The biggest risk is that their dominant position in both finance and industry will give them easy access to public funds, real quasi-fiscal power!

The bank-led FIGs have become the new powerful redistributors of resources in the Russian economy. But, as some may assert, the bank-led FIGs were the only means to acquire, restructure, and sell real value-adding enterprises to create a real market economy. Their long-run prospects, however, are open to question.

The failure of the *keiretsu* in Japan and *chaebols* in Korea (Asian variants of the Russian FIG model) casts doubt on the long-term viability of concentrating financial and industrial assets. *Keiretsu* and *chaebols*, at least initially, did not have a common budget with the government. But they grew to acquire one. The experience of the Czech Republic, in which the government owned the banks, which owned the investment privatization funds, which owned the companies, and which resulted in the failure of microeconomic restructuring of enterprises, has prompted the Czech government to sell its shares in the banks to foreign banks and to break up its FIG model.

It does not make economic sense for banks to have as their chief clients for loans the firms they own. The incentives are wrong. Banks can often earn higher profits by lending to their industrial subsidiaries than by restructuring those firms into profitable enterprises. What may be good for the banks is not good for the broader economy. The development of real banks in Russia is going to require that FIGs give way to a separation of banking from real commercial and industrial activities.

With this background, let us consider the balance sheet of the banking system as of December 1, 1997. The "standard" balance sheet that appears in table 4, when compared with its counterpart in table 1 for the end of 1995, appears to show a dramatic improvement in the health of the banking system. Total assets appear to have increased more rapidly than total liabilities, doubling the equity of the banks (even after adjusting for inflation). Nonborrowed reserves also appear to have nearly doubled. Thus the standard balance sheet implies that great progress was made during 1996–1997 in improving the solvency and liquidity of the banking system.

The "revised" balance sheet for December 1, 1997, table 5, tells an entirely different story. Negative nonborrowed reserves increased sixfold compared with their counterpart in table 2 for the end of 1995, which means that liquidity in the banking system had further deteriorated. As to solvency, both assets and liabilities nearly doubled during 1996–1997, but the banks remained in

Table 4. Standard Balance Sheet of Russian Commercial Banks as of December 1, 1997 (all values in billions of current rubles)

Assets		*Liabilities*	
Reserves	62,884	Demand deposits	121,143
Foreign assets	82,484	Time deposits	105,745
Claims on the government	188,186	Foreign exchange deposits	77,898
Claims on enterprises (performing loans)	289,423	Government deposits	30,150
Claims on other financial institutions	497	Central Bank credit	10,527
		Bank-issued bills of exchange, equal to quasi–Central Bank credit	20,361
Undistributed assets	2,190	Foreign liabilities	115,113
		Undistributed liabilities	0
Total Assets	625,664	Total Liabilities	480,937
Memorandum item: bank liquidity (nonborrowed reserves)	52,357	Equity	144,727

Table 5. Revised Balance Sheet of Russian Commercial Banks as of December 1, 1997 (all values in billions of current rubles)

Assets		*Liabilities*	
Reserves and CB deposits	62,884	Demand deposits	121,143
Reserves	36,200	Time deposits	105,745
CB deposits	26,684	Foreign exchange deposits	77,898
Foreign assets	85,484	Government deposits	30,150
Claims on the government	188,186	Central Bank credit	10,527
All claims on enterprises (performing) (equities, loans issued as bank bills of exchange, performing money loans)	273,098	Bank-issued bills of exchange, equal to quasi– Central Bank credit	37,226
Equities (market value)	100,000	Foreign liabilities	115,113
Loans issued as bank bills of exchange	37,226	Bank bonds (tradeable)	9,733
Money loans (performing)	135,872	Undistributed liabilities	0
Nonperforming loans (principal) (for information only)	(25,053)	Loans to bank-owned enterprises (estimated)	65,000
Nonperforming loans (interest) (for information only)	(25,912)	Contingent liabilities: direct government loans to bank-owned enterprises (est.)	8,000
Claims on other financial institutions	497	Contingent liabilities: tax arears (est.)	60,000
Undistributed assets	2,190	Contingent liabilities: payroll arears (est.)	10,000
Total Assets	609,339	Total Liabilities	650,535
Memorandum item: bank liquidity (nonborrowed reserves)	(11,553)	Equity	(41,196)

even a more negative equity position than two years before. The ratio of assets and liabilities to equity, however, markedly deteriorated during 1996–1997. Put another way, the banking system generated a significant increase in credits on a zero capital base. The Russian financial system is, to put it mildly, living danger-

Table 6. Monetary Survey, Balance Sheet of the Central Bank of
Russia and the Commercial Banks (billions of rubles)

	1/1/96	*1/1/97*	*7/1/97*	*1/1/98*
Assets				
Net foreign assets	70,223	49,335	84,563	7,225
Domestic credit	363,673	539,298	580,915	669,414
Claims on the government	166,588	311,467	328,805	378,856
By commerical banks	62,639	150,721	187,093	191,078
By CBR	103,949	160,746	141,712	187,778
Claims on enterprises	196,570	227,589	252,011	390,548
Claims on non-banks	525	242	100	9
Liabilities				
Money	151,267	192,402	242,496	269,362
Currency	80,800	103,800	136,900	130,500
Demand deposits	70,467	88,602	105,596	138,862
Quasi-money	124,513	164,922	180,760	189,570
Bank bills of exchange	11,859	30,372	23,882	27,896
Other liabilities	46,489	22,940	16,522	(29,759)
Equity	99,768	177,996	201,820	219,572
Memorandum items				
Net domestic assets	68,100	123,000	106,100	141,200
Net international reserves,				
$ million	7,700	1,700	11,000	4,200
Monetary Base	103,800	130,900	167,000	164,500
M_2 (includes banks with				
revoked licenses)	220,800	295,200	363,800	384,500
M_2 (excludes banks with				
revoked licenses)	220,800	288,300	352,000	370,200

Source: Central Bank of Russia, various releases.

ously at the public expense as it creates a hazard for the fiscal
system. These circumstances explain why the entire credit structure came perilously close to collapse at the end of 1997 as the
ruble came under pressure and why the CBR had to defend the
ruble at all costs.

Table 6 presents an IMF-style monetary survey, which com-
bines the assets and liabilities of the Central Bank of Russia with

those of the commercial banks. Looking at tables 4, 5, and 6, let us review the major trends in the banking system during 1996–1997.

As we have said many times, any apparent expansion of bank credit is not due to the creation of deposits as in normal commercial banking systems. In Russia, a principal source of financing economic activity in 1996–1997 was the creation of money by the CBR as it repurchased, or recycled, government debt. An increasingly important source of financing in 1997 was the creation of rubles by the CBR as it bought up foreign capital inflows with newly created rubles.

In 1996, the CBR repurchased short-term debt from the banks and banks capitalized high rates of interest in (paper) equity. CBR claims on the government increased from R104 trillion to R161 trillion, or 55 percent, during 1996. That R57 trillion increase in debt repurchase led to an increase of R55 trillion in net domestic assets. That monetary expansion sparked an inflation scare and nearly depleted foreign exchange reserves, as holders of rubles perceived that the exchange-rate band could no longer be sustained at the end of 1996.

The new monetary system of 1995–1996 effectively replicated the previous regime of direct CBR credit to the government and the banks, except that the new regime securitized this credit in the form of government bonds, recycled through the banks. The fixed exchange-rate regime helped reduce inflation, but it also constrained the CBR's ability to repurchase debt. As 1996 drew to a close, the new monetary system was on the brink of failure.

In the first half of 1997, the CBR purchased nearly $10 billion of foreign exchange from the banks and the government, issuing rubles in exchange. Those purchases of foreign exchange reflected rising demand for rubles by foreigners. This fresh burst of outside resources enabled the CBR to expand the money supply, keep the banking system liquid, and also preserve the exchange-rate band and the monetary system that was based on it. As previously described, this monetary expansion became possible through the sale of government debt to foreign investors and the serendipity effect of the past privatization and bank recapitalization policies: Banks were cashing in their shares in natural resource enterprises granted by the government to foreign investors. By this time, the Ministry of Privatization, not the CBR, had become Russia's effective monetary authority.

In addition to openly transferring shares in mineral wealth to banks, the Ministry of Privatization also conducted a series of secret swaps of the equity of insolvent banks (an effective partial nationalization) for government equity in oil corporations. That was especially important in late 1995 when, after the rise of interest rates and the liquidity crisis, major banks lacked funds to purchase enterprise shares even at a great discount. One of the most prominent Russian banks, Menatep, was saved this way.[6] The switch from recycling government debt to recycling shares in mineral rights and shifting bank recapitalization to foreign investors could continue while the supply of shares in natural resources lasted. But this means of recapitalizing banks was undermined by the Asian debt crisis as foreign investors fled emerging markets in late 1997. Russia was hit particularly hard: Net foreign assets of the monetary authorities and commercial banks collapsed from nearly $15 billion in mid-1997 to $1.2 billion in January 1998 and then turned negative, rising to more than minus $2 billion in March.

Banking activity in the real economy during 1995–1997 was hardly noticeable. Performing loans increased from R128 trillion in January 1996 to R136 trillion in December 1997, that is,

6. Chrystia Freeland, "Moscow Sold Shares in Oil Companies in Exchange for a Stake in a Commercial Bank," *Finansovye Izvestiia*, no. 10 (February 1, 1996): 1; Gennadi Pisotsky, "The Bank Is Authorized to Swap and Spin," ibid.

declined by 21 percent in real inflation-adjusted terms. The share of performing loans in bank assets fell during this period from 41 percent to 22 percent. The share of government debt in bank assets increased from 8 percent in January 1995 to 20 percent in January 1996 to 31 percent in December 1997 and far exceeded performing loans to enterprises by 38 percent. The volume of government debt in bank assets more than tripled during 1996–1997 and ended up in the growth of banks' paper equity. Banks did not mobilize the savings of the population and did not create additional deposits. They simply automatically multiplied CBR additions to the monetary base. The ratio of M_2 to cash hovered at three to one, in marked contrast to the ratio of ten to one or more in Western market economies.

Veksels

In addition to all the other problems we have described for Russian banks, there is another: bills of exchange or promissory notes. Russian banks have issued a growing stock of private bills of exchange, or promissory notes, named *veksels* after the German bills of exchange of the nineteenth century. *Veksels* work as follows. Russian banks extend loans to enterprises in the form of private bills of exchange. These banknotes resemble large, lump-sum checks. They are redeemable in cash by the issuing bank at a particular date. In the meantime, the notes circulate like regular money, being endorsed and passed along from one holder to another. *Veksels* are generally used only among enterprises and other businesses, not by individuals. Their credibility is not backed by some hard assets of the issuing bank set aside as cover for notes; rather, their credibility rests on the public's willingness to accept them as a means of payment.

Banks began to issue *veksels* in substantial amounts after the fixed exchange-rate regime was put into place, which reduced the

issue of CBR credit and created a liquidity squeeze. *Veksels* replaced the CBR accommodation in liquidity with self-liquidity.
Banks do not place reserves with the CBR for the right to issue
veksels. The interest rate of *veksels*, at the end of 1997, was in
the neighborhood of 40 percent.

The problem with *veksels* is that, in Russia's financial system,
they are another form of direct or indirect quasi-CBR credit. The
CBR regulates the total amount of *veksels* that can be issued and
which banks can issue them. In those regulations, the CBR im-
plicitly ensures the convertibility of *veksels* into real credit, the
equivalent of real money.

In comparing table 5 with table 2, we see that the quantity of
veksels more than doubled during 1996–1997, amounting to
about 6 percent of bank liabilities on December 1, 1997. That
sum, by itself, exceeds the value of bank reserves held with the
CBR (R37 trillion and R36 trillion, respectively). *Veksels* have
made the structural illiquidity of the banking system worse.

Corporations have also issued *veksels*, which trade at a much
higher premium than bank-issued *veksels*. One reason is that
corporate *veksels* are not necessarily redeemable in cash, but
rather in kind in some instances, and that corporate finances are
even shakier than those of the banks.

In addition to bank- and corporate-issued *veksels*, cities and
regional governments also issue their own private money. Together, they amounted, at the end of 1997, to R350 trillion, nearly
three times the ruble currency in circulation. *Veksels* complicate
the task of building a real monetary system by adding liabilities
to the country's financial system and putting the banks at higher
risk.[7]

---

7. Adam Smith wrote over two centuries ago about the "fictitious bills of
exchange" drawn and redrawn between banks and enterprises in larger and
larger amounts. Since there are no real "debtors" behind these bills, they are
eventually redeemed by the Bank of England. This "artful contrivance" ruins

SUMMARY

The recycling first of government bonds and then of privatized natural wealth kept the financial system afloat but failed to produce real growth. All that really happened was that the government subsidized banks—to do what? The hope was that subsidized banks would transmit subsidies to enterprises, as they had done under the monetary policy of directed credit and high inflation of 1992–1994. The story during 1995–1997 was that the government subsidized banks, which bought government debt, which was used to finance subsidies to the banks. The real economy was nowhere to be found in that equation. As a result, enterprises, which were deprived of the flows of monetary accommodations of enterprise arrears through bank credit as in earlier years, switched to self-accommodation through building up tax arrears (further compounding the government debt problem). By various official counts, the stock of enterprise tax arrears to the consolidated budget grew from 3 percent of GDP in 1994 to more than 20 percent in early 1998.[8] Tax arrears increased the budget deficit; financing the deficit through high-yield bonds increased government debt. This was a continuous double fiscal trap. The true underlying financing of this fiscal regime stemmed from implicit tax increases, such as payroll arrears and rising user fees on utilities, as well as from central bank seigniorage, including the continuous inflation tax.

Russia did not have normal fiscal and banking systems during

"public credit" and the monetary system and brings on "the distress of the country." Adam Smith, *An Inquiry into the Nature and Causes of the Wealth of Nations* (London: T. Nelson and Sons, 1895), pp. 127–28.

8. According to the State Tax Service (the Russian equivalent of the U.S. Internal Revenue Service), the consolidated tax arrears of enterprises reached R554.9 billion, or 21 percent of GDP in February 1998 (*Finansovye Izvestiia*, February 24, 1998). Of this amount, R297.9 billion is owed to the federal budget excluding social trust funds. Those numbers include fines and penalties.

1996–1997. A normal monetary system could not exist under such conditions, even if the central monetary authority appeared to have real instruments of monetary policy. Real fiscal and banking systems, the anchor of monetary policy, are essential to the conduct of a fixed or quasi-fixed exchange-rate regime. In the absence of fiscal and banking systems, what began in the second half of 1995 as a monetary regime based on a fixed exchange rate ended up in 1997, remarkably, as a quasi–currency board regime based on government grants of natural wealth to banks and their resale of mineral rights to foreign investors. Such a regime was impermanent from the start because mineral rights, once sold to foreigners, cannot be recycled.

The Asian contagion highlighted the fragility of this regime. As foreign investors began to cash out at the end of 1997, the CBR was forced to let interest rates rise to persuade Russians and foreigners to hold rubles. A devaluation of the ruble would have ended the incipient monetary regime that the government had worked so hard to maintain. CBR sales of dollars, to preserve the exchange-rate band, contracted the monetary base in early 1998. The monetary system thus hung in the balance as the authorities sought out new sources of foreign capital—foreign loans, additional IMF grants.

CHAPTER FOUR

Will Russia Maintain Its Emerging Monetary System and Develop Real Banks? 1998 and Beyond

As demonstrated in chapter 3, the emergence of a real monetary system in Russia stemmed from the pressure of the IMF and other international creditors and some perhaps lucky happenstance. In any event, the CBR lost its freedom to issue credits to the central and regional governments and to enterprises. Rather, it began to behave as a real central bank through the issue of currency, the regulation of banks, open market operations (even if its repurchase of bonds was excessive), and setting its refinancing rate close to the market rate of interest.

WILL RUSSIA MAINTAIN ITS TRIAL MONETARY SYSTEM?

Does the chairman of the CBR (and for that matter the president, prime minister, and first deputy prime ministers) understand the principles of money and banking that are taught in introductory economics courses? There is no way to be certain. Have he and his fellow directors (along with the top government officials) learned how to operate the standard tools of monetary policy in a way that will bring about price stability and create an economic climate conducive to growth? Or is the CBR simply captive to changing economic and financial circumstances, temporarily restricted by international arrangements from full freedom of action.

There is anecdotal evidence that the CBR is still learning about monetary policy and management. For example, it tried to simultaneously maintain its low refinance rate and defend the ruble as foreign reserves drained from the system in early December 1997. It took a private Western investment banker, Renaissance Capital's Boris Jordan, to explain to the CBR that it could not fix two levers of monetary policy simultaneously. Even his elementary arguments were not persuasive until $5 billion in reserves drained abroad within the short span of a week and the entire banking system was on the verge of collapse. Foreign liabilities of all domestic banks substantially exceeded their foreign assets at the prevailing exchange rate, and any ruble devaluation would have dramatically increased the ruble value of their net foreign liabilities.

As long as Russia depends on the IMF, the World Bank, and other international creditors for financial support, the CBR is likely to function as a normal monetary authority and defend the ruble within an acceptable exchange-rate band. If and when the Russian government decides that it no longer requires international aid, and therefore need not adhere to IMF monetary and fiscal targets, the government could instruct the CBR to issue new credits. The jury is still out on this question.

It is important to trace the path through which the Russian government achieved internal financial stabilization, that is, financed its deficits. The method was to issue and roll over short-term, high-yield government bills and bonds, not a sustainable practice over the long run. During the past few years, and into early 1998, both foreign and domestic (largely Russian banks) investors required high yields to hold government debt (in part, reflecting a fear of ruble devaluation).

A vicious circle thus developed. As the cost of servicing government debt continued to mount, and as it had to be rolled over given its short-term maturity, the government continued to inject real assets, at subsidized prices, into restoring the depleted true capital of Russian banks.

The solution, of course, was to eliminate deficits through more rigorous tax enforcement and elimination of numerous direct and hidden subsidies, including self-subsidies in the form of tax arrears. However, aggressive tax enforcement, forcing Russian banks to pay the tax liabilities of their enterprises, has resulted in the banks' occasionally threatening to dump bonds to the government's peril.

Here is where banking reform and a more stable, solvent government go together. The CBR can instruct the banks to submit their true balance sheets, which would include all comprehensive liabilities, including the tax arrears of enterprises owned by banks. The simple rationale for this request would be to check the banks' capital adequacy. When all hidden liabilities (bank-issued bills of exchange, enterprise tax arrears, enterprise payroll arrears, etc.) are included, and all hidden but nonviable assets (nonperforming loans, etc.) are subtracted, most banks, including the major banks, would be revealed as insolvent.

With full balance sheets in hand, the CBR could start the process of reform by, first and foremost, swapping banks' liabilities with the government (tax arrears of enterprises) for the banks' claims on the government (bond holdings). The government would recover its bonds instead of repurchasing them, thereby greatly reducing the internal debt and debt service costs. That would dramatically relieve the strain on the public finances as it cased pressure on the ruble.

The fiscal position of the government would become much

healthier because both the size of the debt and future debt service costs would be reduced. The monetary position would be healthier because dependence on foreign investors to buy public debt would diminish and the threat of their fleeing would subside. The real economy would be healthier as interest rates came down. And the banking system would be healthier as the banks' balance sheets were cleaned up, allowing the central bank to implement a comprehensive banking reform. We now turn to delineating such a reform.

DEVELOPING REAL BANKS: A PROPOSAL FOR REFORM

There is one piece of good news. In the first week of January 1998, the Russian government gave its initial approval to two major U.S. banks (Bank of America and J.P. Morgan) and two major German banks (Deutsche Bank and Commerzbank) to open subsidiaries in Russia. Those four were among twenty foreign banks that had applied for licenses to set up subsidiaries. Although several foreign banks had operated offices in Russia that focused on business such as financing trade deals, the new subsidiaries would be permitted to engage in full-scale, domestic banking operations.

The full details of their operations will become clear with time. Ideally, the foreign subsidiaries will be able to engage in unrestricted retail branch banking, accept deposits from the public, and make commercial and consumer loans in both rubles and foreign currency. Foreign subsidiary banks differ from FIG-centered banks in that the growth of their business depends on the real demand for money, not on government assistance. Such a development would help transform Russian ersatz banks into real banks. It is hoped that all twenty foreign banks and more will be permitted to open full-scale operations in Russia in the near future.

At the beginning of 1998, however, foreign banks only represented about 4 percent of all banking capital in Russia. As a result, the growth of real credit, and real economic activity, will still depend on Russian commercial banks for the next few years. It is important, then, to consider how Russian banks might be reformed to help finance growth.

A Modest Proposal

The objective of bank reform is to build a new banking system of private credit markets. In the new system, depositors should be able to place their savings in new, private, independent, well-capitalized domestic and foreign banks. This process requires an orderly transformation of the banking system and the bankruptcy of insolvent banks.

In a nutshell, the proposal involves the swap of assets, of debt for equity, with the following constituent elements.

The federal and regional governments need to establish *funds* owned by various groups of holders of the governments' internal debt—for example, depositors of the state Savings Bank who lost their savings during the big inflation of the early 1990s. Other holders of implied government liabilities include those Russian citizens with claims on current and future government expenditures (e.g., members of the municipal housing queues, pensioners, households entitled to free or subsidized health care and education, and so forth). *These funds can be capitalized with real assets,* such as natural resources, pipelines, forests, and municipal and agricultural land, among others.

Although in recent years the government gave away a large amount of valuable assets in subsidies to bankers and other preferred interests, the government still owns big stakes (hundreds of billions of dollars) in the natural gas and oil industries, their pipelines, the power industry, and so on. Vacant municipal land for housing development is still largely untapped. These *real* assets could be swapped for both the current and the future liabilities of the federal and regional governments to groups such as those listed above. Swapping real assets for debt liabilities using this formulation would create new institutional investors with real assets and, at the same time, reduce or eliminate future government liabilities by reducing the stream of fiscal expenditures on social programs. In effect, the swap would privatize publicly financed social programs.

How would such a swap include a banking reform? The newly capitalized funds could establish new banks and either replace or take over existing insolvent banks. The existing debt of the commercial banks, whether to the Central Bank or the Savings Bank, would be privatized to—become the liability of—the owners of the new funds (and banks); in return, the new funds/banks would acquire the equity of the indebted commercial banks. The swap or exchange process would include the Savings Bank, which would also be privatized to the new funds/banks and their depositors, who would assume the liabilities of the Savings Bank in exchange for its equity.

To clean up the mess that now characterizes the ersatz banks, which masquerade as real banks in Russia, a high priority is ensuring that their balance sheets during the private takeover process reveal the extent of each institution's insolvency. In particular, nonperforming loans should be subtracted from assets and set aside in escrow. In addition, bank-issued *veksels* should be added to their liabilities. Properly speaking, the banks should be forced to set aside—as a reserve requirement with the Central Bank—the entire value of these promissory notes (liabilities), the financial equivalent of travelers checks, insofar as they represent the equivalent of implicit Central Bank credit (becoming explicit if and when monetized).

The markets would then select those banks that are to survive under the new private ownership arrangements, thereby directing an orderly bankruptcy process. Swapping debt for equity would thus prevent bank failures, closures, panic runs on banks, the depreciation of the currency (with its concomitant inflation), and the further contraction of real credit (thereby preventing further economic contraction).

The takeover of indebted and insolvent banks would amount to a wholesale true privatization of the banking industry and, equally important, separate the commercial banks from the government and the common budget. After the swap, the new owners would exchange the nonperforming debt of enterprises, which had been set aside in escrow, for part of their equity. The new banks would become shareholders in enterprises but in a manner completely different from current FIG arrangements. The difference would lie in the fact that the new banks and the enterprises in which they acquired equity (in exchange for nonperforming loans) would no longer have access to government subsidies or subsidized CBR credit.

Our approach differs from that often proposed in both the academic and the popular literature, namely, to write off nonperforming loans and recapitalize banks at government expense. That approach has become especially prevalent in light of the financial crisis that emerged in Asia during the second half of 1997. Our objection to such an approach is that it subsidizes both inefficient enterprises and inefficient banks at a huge cost to taxpayers. Moreover, it invites future mismanagement, if not malfeasance. Rich countries with strong fiscal systems, such as the United States or Japan, may be able to afford such waste, but Russia is much too poor to attempt this strategy.

The debt for equity swap we propose has several desirable

features. It would establish efficient ownership, secure stakes in enterprises, and achieve corporate control in firms whose shares the new funds/banks would choose to keep as a source of income. To the extent that any of the acquired enterprises are profitable, the profits provide resources on which to generate new credit. The new institutional bank owners would have little interest in rolling over the debt of insolvent enterprises. They would be unwilling to risk their good capital, endowed by the government in exchange for canceled entitlements, just to keep bad capital from liquidation. It never makes sense to throw good money after bad. Those new financial institutions should resell their enterprise equity on the market and use the proceeds to invest in profitable activities or use their liquidity for making profitable loans. The new incentives will break up, once and for all, the common budget chain linking the government, banks, and enterprises under the existing arrangements.

The new system would be directed toward maximizing market-earned profit for shareholders, resulting in the direction of credit and investment to profit-maximizing companies and growth-generating household purchases. Because banks would have municipal land in their initial capital and be able to sell it through mortgages, a private housing sector would emerge and construction would contribute to economic growth.

As discussed earlier, the debt/equity swap should also include the swap of bank assets (heavily in government bonds) for bank liabilities (tax arrears owed by bank-owned firms and other debts to the government and the Central Bank) and the swap of bank equity to which those assets correspond. During this process, the government would reduce the amount of its short-term outstanding debt, along with the fiscal costs of debt service. The government would then have the breathing space to replace high-yielding, short-term debt with a spread of longer-maturity debt instruments, as found in most normal market economies, thereby further reducing fiscal outlays.

Stretching out the maturities of government bonds could be part of the debt/equity swap agreement with the new institutional owners. The government could replace the existing stock of short-term public debt with a spread of maturities. Recall that banks experienced a sharp reduction in their income between the middle of 1996 and the end of 1997 as interest rates dramatically declined. Indeed, were it not for a rapid rise in the value of equities held by banks, the entire banking system would have come perilously close to collapse. A more even spread of variable-length government bonds would help smooth out the interest earnings of bonds held in bank vaults. It would also, at crunch time, reduce the pressure on the government to find another way to inject fresh assets into the banks whenever their earnings fell in the face of declining bond yields. A gradual replacement of short-term Treasury bills with long-term bonds as a source of bank assets, on which banks can generate credit, would not cost the government or the taxpayer additional resources.

Let's be clear about what the debt/equity swap would accomplish. When the new system is fully mature, the Central Bank of Russia will be an independent monetary institution and will no longer bear any implicit fiscal liabilities. The ruble note issue, the CBR's currency liabilities, will be backed by the exchange-rate value of its net international reserves and the reality of a growing economy, generating higher output and foreign exchange earnings.

To complete the financial system, the commercial banks will develop a portfolio of assets (loans) backed by the real resources they secured from the government in the debt/equity swap and by their holdings of more-stable, long-term government bonds (which works to the benefit of both the government and the banks).

The system as a whole will take on currency board–like characteristics, rather than remain a fiat system limited solely by international dictates. The CBR will be constrained in its note issue by law and by its need to hold sufficient international reserves to maintain a stable exchange rate. The commercial banks will be constrained in their credit creation by the value of the real resources at their disposal and by the need to earn a positive rate of return on their loans (since government subsidies will no longer be available to make up for losses). Credit will grow in line with profitable, productive economic activities.

To summarize, banking reform and the establishment of private credit markets simultaneously achieve a costless rescheduling of internal debt and diminish a perilous fiscal crisis. Taken together, the process creates a market-based banking system, an independent monetary system, and a more solvent, less debt-burdened fiscal system in one fell swoop.

In the best of all possible worlds, the newly established funds and banks should be run by foreign managers. In fact, the new institutional owners are likely to seek out foreign managers for their integrity and professional skills. After all, Russian bankers are deeply distrusted by the Russian public. The evidence is stark: Russian households hold $40 billion or more in no-interest-bearing American dollar bills. In contrast, interest-earning household deposits in Russian banks are well below their private dollar hoards, and most of those sit in the safer state Savings Bank.

The principal objective of a banking system should be the mobilization of domestic savings for capital formation. If the Russian public begins to own banks through private institutional funds, and begins to trust their new managers, households would begin to convert their dollar hoards into interest-bearing ruble deposits.[1] Such a conversion would strengthen the ruble and

---

1. If the political climate were right, Russia could grant *legal currency status*

greatly increase the available credit for firms and households (e.g., home mortgages). Deposit multiplication through the banking system would increase capital formation. After an initial confidence-building period, the flow of regular savings from income would continuously expand credit and investment.

Another incentive and risk reduction for mobilizing deposits (getting dollars from mattresses) could be dollar-denominated convertible accounts. Under this scheme, deposits could be directly backed by equity shares in natural resource firms and be freely convertible on demand at the stock market rate. Depositors could be paid either interest or dividends, as they desire. In reality, this operation cuts through exchange and brokerage transactions but, if done within the same bank, ensures depositors' confidence.

The government could lend some of its natural resource shares to the Central Bank in exchange for purchasing dollars from the banks' convertible accounts. The Central Bank could then repurchase dollar-denominated government bonds from foreigners (to avert a run on the ruble) and remit the bonds to the government, thereby canceling its resource loan. This short-term measure could reduce the country's short-term foreign debt exposure. It would also allow the CBR to build up foreign exchange reserves at the long-term market value of assets.

---

to the U.S. dollar, which would allow banks to accept dollar deposits and make dollar loans on a coequal contractual basis with rubles. In that event, both the ruble and the dollar would circulate as *official* currencies, as is the case with the peso and dollar in Argentina. In the current climate, Russian households are not likely to trust their dollars to Russian banks. The government would have to authorize foreign banks to open branches in Russia on a broad scale, and those foreign banks would probably have to guarantee, by recourse to assets in their home countries, the dollar deposits placed with them. Russia is probably not ripe for such a reform, given that it recently de-dollarized the economy. But allowing dual currencies to circulate would help ensure the stability of the ruble, as any departure from operating a sound monetary system would cause a shift from rubles to dollars.

Also, the government could place additional equity in natural resources in its own accounts in banks to be exchanged for the dollar-denominated convertible accounts when households deposit their dollar savings. This would eliminate the need for the government to sell assets at a discount to foreign investors to acquire dollars to support the currency and finance its budget deficit. Or, if depositors prefer to hold interest-earning dollar deposits instead of equity shares, their money could be placed in trust with the Central Bank. This would amount to private ownership of that part of CBR reserves of foreign exchange. Either option would secure the stability of the monetary base, reduce the need for new currency issue, and thereby minimize future currency crises.

It can be argued that this proposed reform, while economically rational, is not politically feasible. The structure of interests that has developed between the government and the FIGs is likely to resist any diminution of its financial or political control. Still, the proposal indicates a path open to Russian authorities should the FIG model, the banks, or the currency collapse in the near future. The Russian public would surely favor this reform.

If Russia fails to develop real banks in the near future, we doubt that the Russian economy or its people are likely to enjoy the benefits of sustained growth anytime soon. There may be other ways or modifications of our approach that would also improve the prospects for growth. But repeated hortatory claims about so-called market reforms and *The Coming Russian Boom* have thus far failed to produce growth. Nor have these claims provided constructive options for Russia's people or its policy makers. It's time to come forth with fresh ideas. This volume is a step in that direction.

POSTSCRIPT

What does the future portend if Russia fails to establish real independent banks? The starting point of Russia's commercial banking system is that each bank, apart from the state Savings Bank, has faced a daily scramble to survive since its birth. This book describes how the government has resorted to multiple, creative, direct, and indirect means of injecting fresh assets into the country's ersatz banks to make them appear solvent and liquid. All these means—whether it be Central Bank accommodation of interenterprise credit, high-yield government bonds, low equity transfer prices, resale of equity to foreign investors, IMF loans, eurobonds, or the issue of bank and corporate *veksels*—have something in common. They rest, ultimately, on the transfer of real wealth from the country at large to the banks and their industrial partners or holdings.

The wealth and income of Russia currently derive from its vast stock of oil, gas, minerals, timber, and other natural resources. Since 1991, the government has been drawing down its sources of wealth to sustain the banks, in the hope of jump-starting growth, by transferring control over an increasing share of these assets to a handful of favored, privileged firms and, in lesser degree, to foreigners. Once the government has privatized the last of its natural resource firms, it will have exhausted its ownership of real resources and its ability to continue to furnish new sources of capital to the banks.

It is this process of fresh asset injections that has kept the banks in business even though they have been collectively insolvent and illiquid at virtually every point in time. But the government will soon run out of assets to inject. To make matters worse, in the year 2000, the Russian government will have to begin repaying the IMF in amounts larger than it expects to receive.

Table 7 provides an overview of Russia's financial system as

Table 7. International Solvency and Liquidity of the Russian Financial System, January 1998 (claims on foreign assets without foreign debt to the former Soviet Union denominated in nonconvertible currency against foreign claims on Russian assets) ($ billion)

	FISCAL AUTHORITY			MONETARY AUTHORITY			COMMERCIAL BANKS			CORPORATE SECTOR AND SUBNATIONAL GOVERNMENTS			TOTAL		
	Total	Long term	Short term	Total	Long term	Short term	Total	Long term	Short term	Total	Long term	Short term	Total	Long term	Short term
Assets															
Total	150.8	132.3	18.5	21.3	3.5	17.8	11.3	3.4	7.9	5.0	3.0	2.0	37.6	9.9	27.7
Reserve assets				17.8		17.8							17.8		17.8
Currency				12.9		12.9							12.9		12.9
Gold				4.9		4.9							4.9		4.9
Nonreserve assets				3.5	3.5		11.3	3.4	7.9				14.8	6.9	7.9
Equity (est.)										5.0	3.0	2.0	5.0	3.0	2.0
Liabilities															
Total	150.8	132.3	18.5	13.3	0.2	13.6	18.1	3.7	14.4	30.5	30.0	0.5	212.7	166.2	46.5
Loans (including eurobonds)	134.5	130.5	4.0	13.1		13.6	18.1	3.7	14.4	4.0	3.5	0.5	169.7	137.7	32.0
Bonds (GKO and OFZ)	16.3	1.8	14.5										16.3	1.8	14.5
Other				0.2	0.2								0.2	0.2	
Stocks and corporate bonds (est.)										26.5	26.5*		26.5	26.5	
Net	-150.8	-132.3	-18.5	8.0	3.3	4.2	-6.8	-0.3	-6.5	-25.5	-27.0	1.5	-175.1	-156.3	-18.8

*Quasi long term

Source: Russian Central Bank, various releases   *Note:* Figures may not add due to rounding

of January 1998. The data are segregated into long- and short-term dollar assets and liabilities of the government (fiscal authority), the CBR (monetary authority), the commercial banks, and the corporate sector.[2] On January 1, 1998, net international reserves (NIR) of the Central Bank stood at about $4.2 billion. (By March 1, 1998, net international reserves had fallen to $0.5 billion.) The actual sum of foreign reserves available to the CBR is higher, closer to the published "gross international reserves," or reserve assets, figure. In the table, multiyear IMF loans are counted as short-term liabilities even though most of them are greater than one year in duration and even though IMF repayments due in 1999 and 2000 are likely to be offset by new IMF and World Bank loans.

Thus the bulk of Russia's official gross international reserves, which amounted to just under $18 billion in January 1998, is available to defend the ruble—unless the IMF were to raise objections to running up an official, large, negative "net" position. Breaking an IMF target on the level of NIR is strongly discouraged, although the IMF has let this and other rules slip in the past, when slippage served its convenience. The gross reserves include $4.9 billion in gold, but it is highly unlikely that Russia would or could sell much of its gold reserves overnight, which leaves only $13 billion in liquid gross reserves.

Turning to the commercial banks, their net, short-term foreign liabilities amounted to about $7 billion, a figure that substantially exceeds the CBR's net international reserves. As inflation and interest rates came down, Russian banks headed for the international credit markets en masse. Foreign banks were eager to lend to Russian banks at Libor (London interbank offered rate)

2. Russian holders of dollar accounts in Russian banks are not included in these figures; withdrawals from these accounts do not affect international payments. But they still can add to a currency crisis if the money demand among Russians shifts from rubles to dollars.

plus 3 to 5 percent, given Russia's promising economic prospects. As a result, Russian banks rapidly increased their foreign liabilities in 1997. It was this exposure to the commercial banking system that compelled the CBR to defend the ruble in late 1997 at any cost.

The corporate sector also has net foreign liabilities, consisting largely of $26 billion worth of stock, but most of this can be regarded as quasi long term. It is not possible for foreign investors to sell more than a small chunk of Russian equity for dollars at any point in time. Daily turnover on Russia's stock exchanges is well below $100 million, and most of this volume takes place between domestic buyers and sellers. Foreign holders of equity in Russia are, perforce, in it for the long run whether they like it or not. It is much easier to liquidate bonds and convert the proceeds into dollars than to do the same for equities. Indeed, the corporate sector enjoys positive short-term assets in that its holdings of foreign securities and real estate in Western market economies can be liquidated overnight.

Yet another problem area is the shrinking trade balance, which was running in late 1997 at half (or less) the level of the past few years. Depending on the accuracy of the forecasts, a current-account deficit may occur in 1998. Oil prices are at near record lows. At $13 a barrel, the production of oil for export is no longer profitable for many companies.

The problem that confronts the CBR is, as we have demonstrated, the country's fiscal situation. As of January 1998, $14.5 billion worth of short-term Treasury bills was in foreign hands. To this must be added another $4 billion in short-term loans and eurobonds, putting net short-term foreign liabilities at $18.5 billion. Massive foreign dumping of GKOs is enough to bring the ruble down, which explains why the government raised its refinance rate sharply, from 18 to 42 percent during the latter weeks of 1997 (although it was able to reduce, in several steps, the rate back to 30 percent in mid-March 1998).

If our analysis of the ill health of Russia's financial system is correct, what accounts for a partial decline in interest rates on government debt in the first quarter of 1998 and the success of Russian banks, enterprises, and local governments in raising funds in the eurobond market during the first half of 1998? The nine-month GKO fell to just under 27 percent in a successful auction during the first half of March, even though Moody's downgraded Russian foreign currency debt, both public sector and corporate bonds, to Ba3 on March 11, 1998, saying that Russia remained vulnerable to shock waves from the Asian financial crisis. GKO rates had stood at more than 40 percent in late 1997. In early March 1998, the Moscow City Telephone Network (MGTS in Russian) successfully placed a three-year, $150 million eurobond. The issue was oversubscribed, launched at a price equal to U.S. Treasuries plus 690 basis points (U.S. Treasuries plus 6.9 percent) and was performing well in secondary market trading. That was a remarkable turnaround, as an attempt one week earlier by another Russian firm, Almazy Rossii-Sakha, to place eurobonds fizzled and was withdrawn. Encouraged by MGTS's successful placement in the eurobond market, the federal government raised lira- and deutsche mark–denominated eurobonds during the first four months of 1998.

Russian debt commands a high premium over U.S., European, and other emerging market debt. During the first week of March, for example, Russian sovereign debt was trading at a premium of about 5.4 percentage points over ten-year U.S. dollar-denominated eurobonds. Only Indonesian bonds commanded a higher risk premium among all emerging market debt. The bonds of major Russian banks, such as Uneximbank and Alfa Bank, were trading at anywhere from 1,100 to 1,800 basis points above U.S. Treasuries, compared with smaller spreads of 400 to 490 points during July and September 1997. Russian bank debt is exceptionally high risk, as those spreads indicate.

The Russian debt market is not for the faint of heart. It pays high returns but poses high risk. But in a world of flush global money managers, the amount of money placed in Russian debt, or equities, is literally a drop in the bucket of daily investment allocations. The total value of Russian foreign debt is a tiny fraction of a percentage point of global debt markets. Daily turnover in Russia's stock markets is swamped by daily trading in just one or two U.S. large capitalization stocks. Since money managers are under pressure to secure higher returns in just fractions of a point, placing a tiny portion of their funds in the Russian market appears to be rational.

The increase in the value of U.S. household assets between 1986 and 1996 reveals an explosion in funds looking for higher returns. The U.S. Federal Reserve Board reported that, during those years, GDP increased about 75 percent, while the value of pension assets rose about 180 percent, Treasury securities just under 200 percent, corporate equities about 230 percent, and mutual funds some 370 percent. The value of household assets grew much faster than GDP. A similar pattern—of asset growth exceeding GDP growth—also applies in Europe. All this money has to be put to work somewhere, and global asset allocation is now part of the standard investment decision.

Russia offers higher returns than the lower-risk markets of the United States and Europe. From the standpoint of money managers, it is rational to take a small stake in Russian financial instruments since it holds the promise of higher returns. As events in late 1997 indicated, however, money can flow out of Russia even faster than it comes in.

It is equally rational for Russia's federal government, banks, enterprises, and regional governments to tap the eurobond market. By raising foreign loans, the government can finance its deficit at lower interest rates, which also eases the pressure on domestic ruble interest rates as the government reduces its need to borrow domestically. Russian banks can make productive use of foreign cash by profiting on the difference between foreign and domestic interest rates. Russian enterprises can raise money abroad at cheaper rates than at home. Regional governments need cash any way they can get it. Every domestic player in the Russian economy has an incentive to borrow abroad. Western money managers, flush with cash, are eager to capitalize on the higher spreads of Russian debt and potential higher returns from Russian equities, which is what happened during 1996 and 1997, until the Asian currency crisis spilled over into Russia's financial markets.

As the outstanding stock of Russian foreign debt increases, the system as a whole comes under greater risk, much as happened throughout Asia before the currency crisis that erupted during the second half of 1997. The net short-term debt of the Russian financial system at the start of 1998 was $18.8 billion, owing largely to eurobonds and foreign ownership of domestic bonds (see table 7). As the federal government, regional governments, banks, and enterprises increase their stock of foreign debt, the net short-term liabilities, or exposure, of the financial system increases in tandem. All this debt is explicitly or implicitly guaranteed by the government and the Central Bank. When the next ruble scare erupts, for whatever reason, the pressure on the financial system will be even greater.

Foreign borrowing in and of itself is not necessarily harmful. But it imposes special risks in the case of Russia because there is no real banking system and because the banking system is an integral part of a single financial system combined with the Central Bank and the government (the fiscal authorities). It is exactly this problem that has been the focus of this volume, especially given the country's fiscal situation.

All things considered, the state of Russia's external accounts is, to say the least, precarious, as is the hard-won ruble stability. Total short-term liabilities exceed gross international reserves by a substantial margin. To the extent that the country succeeds in placing large amounts of new foreign bond issues, either by the federal and regional governments or the banks and their enterprises, net short-term foreign liabilities will rise, thus exposing Russia's financial system to even greater risk in the event of a fresh outbreak of the Asian currency crisis. In that event, interest rates would have to rise substantially to defend the ruble.

To the extent that the government is forced to pay high interest to defend the ruble, the banks can continue to remain in business by earning high interest on their government debt, but this will come at the expense of real investment and growth. What might the government do after it runs out of natural resources to transfer to the banks? It might seek to reassert control over some or all of the natural resources previously given to the banks on subsidized terms or devise schemes to recover control over previously privatized oil, gas, and strategic minerals.

Another approach might be to change the flow of funds connected with the export and sale of natural resources, in which the proceeds of sales flow first through the state, leaving the FIGs with the residual claims after the government has extracted whatever share it wishes. This would reverse current practice, in which FIGs secure the earnings and then pay taxes when and if they wish. This second approach nicely fits the model of Moscow mayor Yuri Luzhkov, a prospective candidate for the July 2000 presidential election. The city government is reputed to take a cut of all investment flowing into the Moscow region and a cut in the earnings of Moscow-based enterprises.

A third approach is to force the FIGs to issue shares to the government, which would give it effective control over the proceeds of natural resources. The Moscow City Telephone Network, for example, in early 1998 authorized a 50 percent increase in its shares, which it then transferred to the city government at no charge. This was a further integration of an ostensible private enterprise with a political entity.

It is hard to see where this vicious circle will end, until and unless Russia develops real banks. We have put forth one proposal for such a reform. We welcome others. But the failure to establish real banks in Russia, which remain independent from both the government and the CBR, suggests continued stagnation. Time may be running out on the hard-won existence of the Central Bank if ersatz banks do not give way to real banks in the near future.

THE LAST FOOTNOTE

The flight of foreign capital from Russia in 1998 exposed the extent of the insolvency of the Russian financial system and shattered Russian financial statistics. The combined net foreign assets of the CBR and the commercial banking system fell into the negative column in February 1998, exceeding minus $1 billion, falling to minus $2 billion in March, although they nearly recovered to zero in April. Net international reserves appeared to be zero or even slightly negative in March—a big red flag for the IMF.

As 1998 unfolded, it became technically impossible for the CBR to maintain a consistent set of financial accounts that purported to show a solvent banking system because the CBR found itself in a negative net short-term dollar position. This meant that it could no longer offset the dollar deficiencies of the commercial banks as it, too, was deficient in dollars. At this point, the multiyear pretense of a solvent banking system was no longer important, as the CBR was on the brink of violating its agreements with the IMF. It should be noted that, in selling dollars to protect the ruble within the exchange-rate band, the CBR reduced the stock of domestic currency, thus weakening the balance sheets of the banks. The economy, which in 1997 exhibited feeble signs of bouncing back from a protracted depression, ground to a halt in 1998.

After not disclosing information on the banking sector for a few months in early 1998, the CBR in April 1998 released a new series showing that the true volume of deposits and bank assets was lower than previously reported. The change was due to the fact that the assets and liabilities of defunct banks, whose licenses had been revoked, were now excluded from the revised statistics. Astonishingly, throughout 1997, the CBR had counted in the official series the financial claims of nonexistent banks. The new CBR series also showed that the volume of various bills of exchange in the banks' portfolio of assets, whose real value is overstated, was higher than previously believed. In addition, the CBR ceased publishing the amount of nonperforming loans and other disaggregated data on the banks. These gaps, which it is hoped will be remedied at some future date, would make it possible to apply our revised balance sheet framework to the Russian banking system for the beginning of 1998 and beyond.

However, a few new inferences can be made now. First, the structural insolvency of the banking system is deeper than we documented and reconstructed in tables 2 and 5. Second, the ruble is even shakier than we implied in tables 6 and 7. These revelations render our overall analysis inadvertently optimistic.

The hard-won stability of the Russian currency looks less and less sustainable, not only in the long run but also in the short run. Another global or domestic crisis may bring a devaluation that could reignite inflation and further depress the economy. A reform along the lines we propose, or one with similar objectives in mind, seems no longer to be merely an intellectual exercise but rather a salvaging operation of a country in which the United States and the world have obvious stakes.

ABOUT THE AUTHORS

MICHAEL S. BERNSTAM is a research fellow at the Hoover Institution, Stanford University. He was an economic adviser to the Russian government, the Central Bank of Russia, the Office of the President, and the Parliament on various policy projects in 1991–1995. He coauthored several studies for the World Bank and the U.S. Agency for International Development on reforming Russian energy, banking, and housing industries. He is a regular commentator on Russian economy and finance for Radio Liberty.

ALVIN RABUSHKA is a senior fellow of the Hoover Institution at Stanford University. He is the author or coauthor of numerous books and articles on the economic development of Hong Kong, Taiwan, Singapore, Korea, Malaysia, and China. He writes an annual report on the Israeli economy. He developed, with Robert E. Hall, the flat tax, which was recognized in *Money* magazine's "*Money* Hall of Fame" (1992) for its pioneering contributions to financial innovation. Their most recent work is *The Flat Tax*, 2d ed. (Hoover Press, 1995). During the past few years, he has paid increasing attention to the transition economies of Central and Eastern Europe.

INDEX